Human Space, Stage One

Where You're At
Brian Goodey

Advisory editors
Rex Walford and Michael Storm

Utopia
Colin Ward

Survival
David Wright

Exploration
Margaret Roberts

Maps
Michael Storm

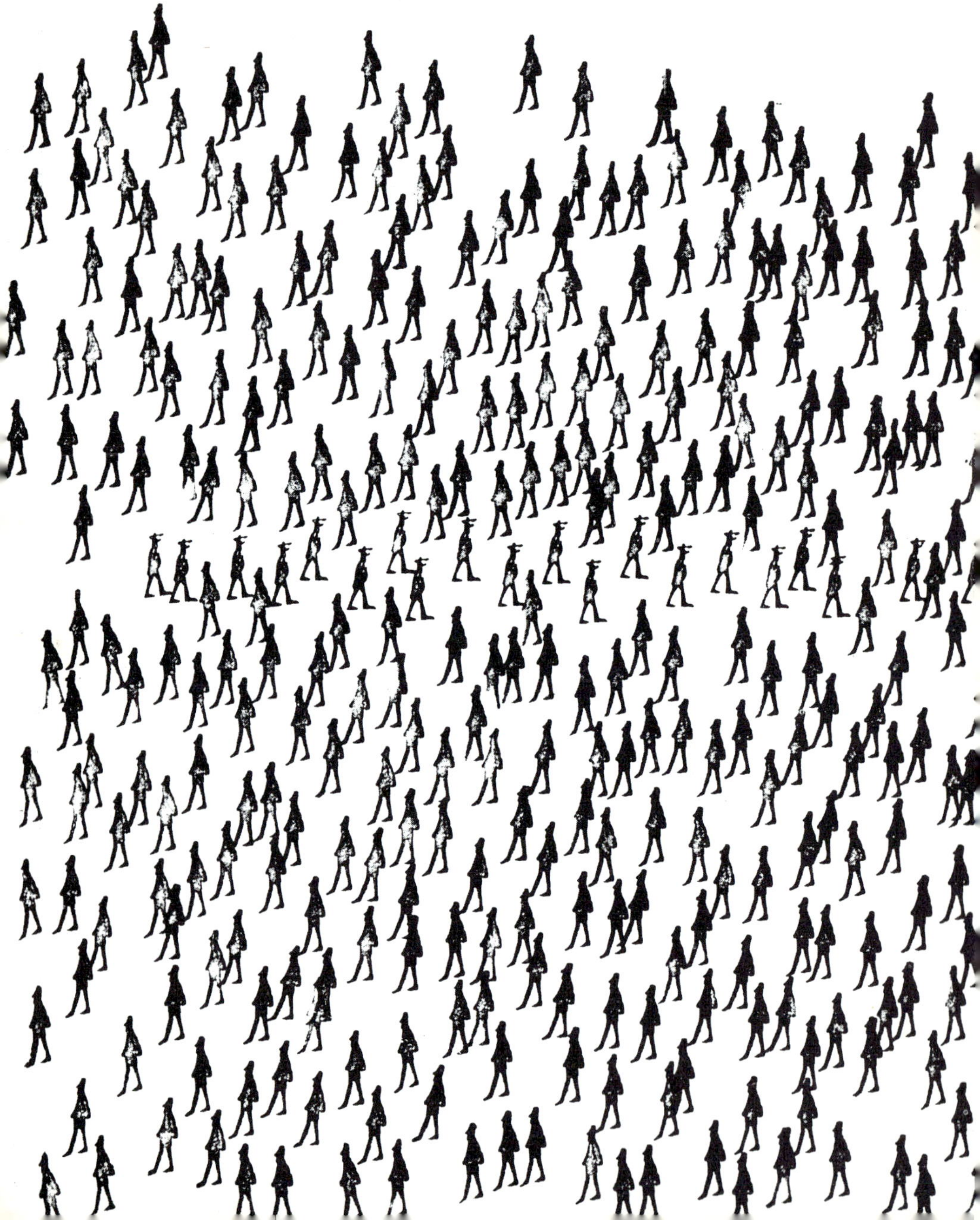

WHERE YOU'RE AT
BRIAN GOODEY

Penguin Education

CONTENTS

Penguin Education,
A Division of Penguin Books Ltd,
Harmondsworth, Middlesex, England
Penguin Books Inc, 7110 Ambassador Road,
Baltimore, Md 21307, USA
Penguin Books Australia Ltd,
Ringwood, Victoria, Australia
Penguin Books Canada Ltd,
41 Steelcase Road West,
Markham, Ontario, Canada

First published 1974
Copyright © Brian Goodey, 1974

Made and printed in Great Britain by
Butler & Tanner Ltd, Frome and London
Set in 11/13 Lumitype Meridien

The author.

BEFORE
YOU BEGIN

Before you begin to use it, a few things about this book.

It's really meant to be *used* and not just read. It's rather thin, but covers a lot of things. As you use it, I hope you'll find some of the gaps and fill them in.

I've tried to suggest some things which might be added or collected, but there is so much information being put out in magazines and newspapers, on television and radio, that I can't really predict what might be useful in the future. That's up to you.

This goes for press cuttings and odd pieces of information you read or see in your own surroundings. Also for pictures which illustrate the book.

This is only a starting point for looking at your local world and the bigger world around it. The book may get stale, but I hope the world doesn't.

1
SPY FLYER

Ben Fox
Industrial Super Spy

*His latest mission - to raid a remote
factory for the secret papers containing
the formula for a revolutionary new process*

7

9

FOLLOW CANAL TO RIGHT OF TOWN ALONG TO TUNNEL

AT TUNNEL LOOK FOR CLEARING IN PINE WOOD WITH GROUP OF TRACTORS AND SMALL CAR STOP LAND HERE STOP TAKE CAR AND RETURN HQ IMMEDIATELY STOP THE BOSS

I'LL CIRCLE DOWN OVER THE CANAL AND LAND IN THE CLEARING

but . .

LOOK ALBERT IT'S ONE OF THEM FLYING SPIES! I'M GOING TO 'PHONE THE POLICE

LEAVE OFF.. YOU'LL DISTURB THE FISH!

These days stories don't often have morals. But if there is one here, it could be that things are not always in the most obvious places.

This book is rather like the story. It's about very important links between us and our surroundings. These are links that are usually so obvious that we don't think much about them.

The story gives some clues to the rest of this book.

PLACES

Most important, this book is about *places* and how you and I identify them. This word *place* is used in many different ways. In the story,

are all places. They may be different shapes and sizes but they do have something in common.

In the story they are all shown in relation to Ben's position. He is *in* the factory and *in* Hemmelig's room. He flies *over* the canal and town.

Places are features – things – in the environment around us by which we work out and describe our own position or the positions of other people and things. Places and people dotted around an area are said to have a *location*, which is usually described in relation to other places. The canal is about a *kilometre away* from the town, the tunnel is *on* the canal, the wood is *beyond* the village . . . these are location-type words. Words that say where things are. Depending on who you are and where you are, places will mean different things, and the more you know of a place, the more detail you can probably give. Ben just had instructions telling him of 'a canal' and 'a small town with a green gasholder'. When he phoned the police, Jim Clun knew that the canal was the 'Little Trunk Canal'.

LABELS

Names such as these, which Jim Clun knew but Ben didn't, are really *labels* for representing places. They are a way of identifying a particular town or a particular canal.

12

Names are the most common form of label — they're usually pretty obvious. We all have one. But we also use many other types of label, including the one on the sauce bottle. In the story David Blair had painted his initials 'D.B.' on his coffee mug — that was a label. Jean Tern had several photographs which served as a label on her desk, linking her with the desk and the desk with her.

There are other labels in the story too, if you look closely. Most rooms which are used by one person — offices, bedrooms, studies, etc. — end up with a number of labels indicating who uses them. Football programmes, pop posters, books, flowers all act as labels in this way. What labels do you use?

OWNERSHIP

Labels usually mean more than the fact that certain people *use* a place, they possibly *own* it as well. The factory in the story was owned by the electronics company. Each room in it was also owned by the company, but certain things, like the coffee mug, belonged to people using the rooms. In Britain, and most of the world today, ownership has become very important, so important that we might think that it is the only thing that matters.

Should everybody own their house and garden? Should the whole country be divided up into pieces owned by individuals? Doesn't this mean that the richest people get the biggest and most important areas because only they can afford to buy them?

There are some pieces of the country — parks, for example — which are *public*. This is supposed to mean that we all own them, but this doesn't seem to work out too well at times.

Not all people believe in the private ownership of land. This is an early European settler in the United States describing his discussion with a group of Indians.

Some travelling Indians having, in the year 1777, put their horses overnight to pasture in my little meadow, at Gnadenhutten on the Muskingum,[1] I called on them in the morning to learn why they had done so. I endeavoured to make them sensible of[2] the injury they had done me, especially as I intended to mow the meadow in a day or two. Having finished my complaint, one of them replied:

'My friend, it seems you lay claim to the grass my horses have eaten, because you had enclosed it with a fence: now tell me, who caused the grass to grow? Can you make the grass grow? I think not, and nobody can except the great Mannitto.[3] He it is who causes it to grow both for my horses and for yours! See, friend! the grass which grows out of the earth is common to all; the game in the woods is common to all. Say, did you never eat venison and bear's meat?'

'Yes, very often!'

'Well, and did you ever hear me or any other Indian complain about that? No; then be not disturbed at my horses having eaten only once, of what you call *your* grass, though the grass my horses did eat, in like manner you did eat, was given to the Indians by the Great Spirit. Besides if you will but consider, you will find that my horses did not eat *all* your grass. For friendship's sake, however, I shall never put my horses in your meadow again!'

John Heckewelder, *Account of the History, Manners and Customs of the Indian Nations*

[1] a river in Ohio, USA [2] tried to explain [3] the Indian's God

BARRIERS

One of the problems about owning things is that if you're really going to make sure that they're yours and no one else's, you have to find ways of stopping other people taking them. How do you do that? And how do other people do it to you?

This plays a big part in the story of Ben Fox. His job was to get things which others owned, and to do so he had to break through a number of *barriers* which had been put up to keep people like him out. Barriers are usually erected to stop people or things getting in or out of somewhere – walls, locked doors, turnstiles, fences. There are probably quite a lot in your local area. Some will be selective, like cattle grids, which act only as barriers to animals. Others, like prison walls, will be almost totally effective. They're interesting things because they can tell you a lot about a place or a situation. When you see barriers, try working out these things: Whose interests or property are they protecting? Who are they trying to keep out, and why?

THE BIGGER THE BETTER?

There's another idea that crops up in the story, and will again in the rest of the book. Did you notice the three offices in the story were different? David's was small and crowded, Jean's was bigger and had a view, and Hemmelig's was large, well-equipped and appeared to have valuable furniture. It's connected with ownership and labels: it seems that the size of a room and the value of its contents are somehow connected

Face to Face   Round the Bend   Out of sight

to the importance of the person using it. David was a junior, Jean in the middle and Hemmelig the senior. The link between the importance of a person and the size of his office is found all over the world; it is very much part of the way we live. The school principal has his own office and more often than not the rest of the staff are crowded in the Staff Room. Do people with power really need larger rooms and more impressive furniture?

HIERARCHY

Lots of things are arranged like this in order of importance or rank: first the smallest or least important, then a slightly bigger one, and so on. This kind of arrangement is known as a *hierarchy*. Hierarchies are sorting systems which are used to classify and to organize people and things. I usually think of those Russian wooden dolls, made like boxes. When you unscrew the head and body you find another doll inside – in fact you find several, all inside each other. A hierarchy is like that, one big thing with a lot of smaller ones inside. Think of the way a company is organized, with a few directors and managers at the top and a lot of men and women at various ranks below them. David, Jean and Hemmelig were part of just such a hierarchy, and their rooms reflected their positions in it. The armed forces and the police are even better examples. There, people at different levels in the hierarchy have different uniforms. The higher up they are, the more colourful and decorative their uniform and the more power they have. Most countries have this way of organizing people, things and places.

Left: these ideas on places, labels, ownership, barriers and hierarchies shouldn't be too strange. We all come across them every day, even if we don't realize it. Some of the ideas have even crept into the way people talk – not just about places, but about the way they feel, too. How many phrases like this can you think of? Try your own cartoons.

2
WHERE YOU'RE AT

How would you describe where
you are at this moment?
At home?
On a bus?
In the classroom?

From left to right along the rows:
each of these pictures shows the
world from ten times further away
than the one before. It's like making
a journey in eight gigantic leaps,
taking off straight upwards from
where you began and out into the
universe. What does each picture
show? Try making your own series.
What would *you* look like from ten
times further away, a hundred times,
a thousand times, ten thousand . . .?

18

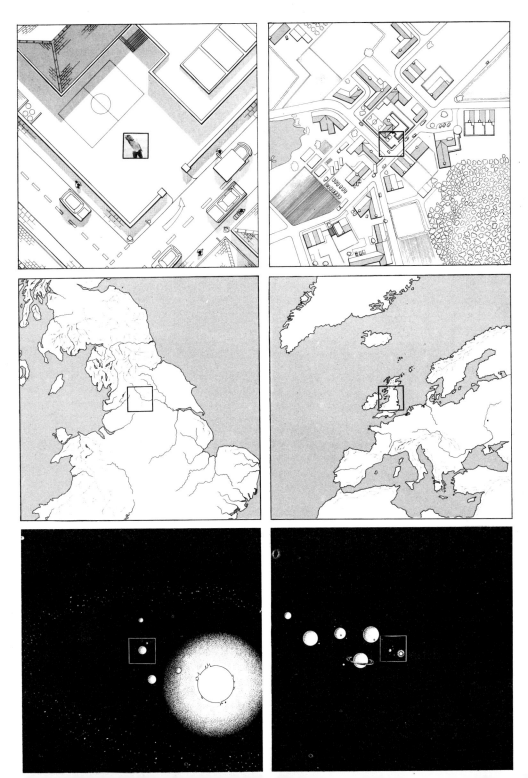

As long as I can remember schoolbooks have had something like this written in their inside covers:

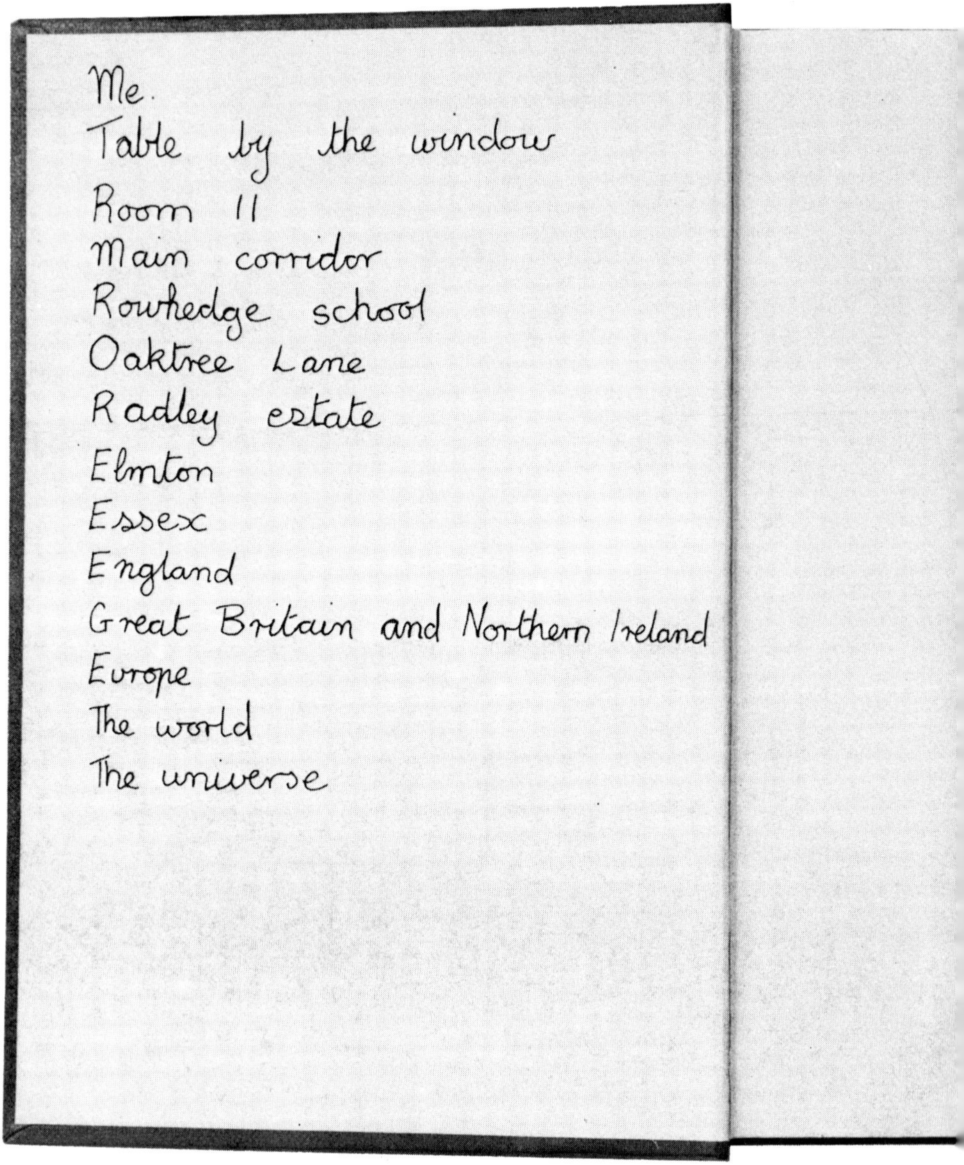

Me.
Table by the window
Room 11
Main corridor
Rowhedge school
Oaktree Lane
Radley estate
Elmton
Essex
England
Great Britain and Northern Ireland
Europe
The world
The universe

I've only seen this done in schoolbooks, but a similar address could be written for anyone – the Queen, David Cassidy, the Pope, your mother.

PAR AVION 航

Chen Mao Chang
4-3, Alley 20. Lone 64
Nonking West- Road
Taipei Taiwan
Rep of China

PRINTED MATTER

Fraulein Susan Orgar
Oelbermannstiftung
Hohenstaufenring 57a
5 Koln
Deutschland

Apartment No. 64
2863 Washington Street
Springfield City
State of Montana
United States of America

Some people's addresses might come out like these. Although the order may be a little different, and some addresses put a lot more details in, the broad pattern is the same. Try addresses of some relatives or famous people.

If you do one of these for 'where you're at', it tells you something about your position in the world. In fact, it places you exactly in the universe. Such an address is yours alone.

Notice how everything you write below your name is bigger than you; all the lines are rather like that Russian doll. You fit in your room, your room and others fit into a corridor, and so on until all the continents, of which Europe is only one, fit into the world. It's another of those hierarchies – a hierarchy of size or scale. You can see it if you draw a picture or a map for each line of the address and mark where the place in the line before fits in.

Apart from identifying who the schoolbook belongs to, an address like this could also be useful for someone who didn't know where you were and wanted to find you. Starting with the largest scale, the last line – the Universe – and with the help of atlases, maps and street plans, they could gradually narrow down your location until they knew exactly where you were. Try it yourself. Any address will do, though it may sometimes be hard to get hold of the street plans you need. There are quite a few addresses in this book that you could try for a start.

Me.
Table by the window
Room 11
Main corridor
Rowhedge school

The first part of the 'address' locates your place in detail: in a building or a field or wherever else you happen to be. Can you collect information on labels, ownership and barriers to fit in with these places?

SMALL SCALE

In a school which is heavily used by a large number of people, you may not have official labels to identify your place. They are not necessary really, but labels are becoming very common in business. This could be so that people 'know their place' and don't get lost in vast new office blocks.

Possibly the use of names and labels printed on desks and doors is to make up for the fact that people don't seem to tell others much about themselves. The bank manager, the vicar and the shopkeeper needn't bother to introduce themselves, they can rely on their painted name-plates to do it for them.

School classrooms have labels, some official and some which are probably only known to you and other students using them. All those carvings and inked initials on desks, for instance.

As a unit – a place – the school as a whole certainly has labels. These include badges, colours, uniforms, printed notepaper from the Head's office, rubber stamps with the school name. There are probably many more that I haven't thought of.

Most organizations go in for this sort of label. Shops use a certain colour scheme and style of lettering for their uniforms. A factory probably marks all of its products with the same trademark – another form of label. Some factories and businesses have coats-of-arms, and this is true of most cities and towns as well.

Some people spend their time designing such things. Industrial and advertising designers draw out samples of trademarks and work out colour

22

schemes. What makes a trademark good or bad? How do these designers think their designs work? Why do they think they're necessary? They're interesting people to talk to, if you can track them down. You could try asking questions at the kind of place where people like this are trained – your local art school for example.

How many different kinds of labels can you find in this picture? Who has put them there and who do you think they're meant for? How has that affected the way they're written? How would you react to them?

When I walk to work it only takes me about ten minutes and there are no factories or shops on the way. You wouldn't expect to see many labels, but I counted twenty business labels when I last looked. House names are cheating, but look for things like fire hydrants and manhole covers, vans passing on the road, badges on uniforms, etc.

KEEP OFF THE GRASS

How many of those labels mark *barriers* at the local level? There are probably ways of indicating the edge of the school. Walls and fences, for example. These also keep people and things in (or out), depending on the time of day, or the time of year. Sometimes barriers are obvious, but often you don't know they exist until somebody shouts at you.

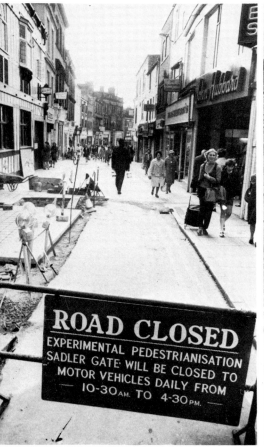

Spot the difference. How effective are the barriers in these pictures and what makes them strong or weak? Would *you* take any notice?

If you start to look at the school and the area around it you'll find a large number of places, owned by other people, which you aren't allowed into.

I tend to think of such barriers as *strong* or *weak*. A weak barrier is a KEEP OFF THE GRASS sign when there's no park-keeper around. This is really no barrier at all, but it gets stronger if the park-keeper comes along. Some of the strongest barriers I've seen are those building sites which have three-metre-high fences plastered with notes telling you that GUARD DOGS ARE PATROLLING!

WHO OWNS YOU?

What about ownership? Who owns the desk, the room and the school? You could argue about this for some time. Different people will give you different answers, but most schools are owned by the local education authority which is supported by taxes from your parents. Private schools can be owned by a single person, though this is not very common. They make money by getting parents to pay fees for their children to go there.

All matters of ownership, however small the area or the building concerned, seem to get very complicated. It would be easy if we could assume that the name on a shop or office building meant that those people owned the building and the land. But things don't work out that way.

Office buildings, especially, are often owned by companies which people know very little about. They rent the space out to other companies and get large amounts of money for doing so. In the same way, a landowner may lend a builder land to build on for a number of years – usually a long time like ninety-nine years. The houses or commercial buildings he builds are known as *leasehold*. This is different from *freehold*. A freehold property is one where the land and the building belong to the same person or can be bought together. The whole business of property tends to get very muddled. A few people make big profits out of it, but lots of others tend to get hurt in the process.

Hump ~ ty Dump ~ ty sat on a wall

The General Electric Company is one of the largest companies in Britain. In 1972 it had 181,000 people working for it and made a profit of £77 million. All the factories and offices pictured here, and lots of others besides, belong to GEC; but would you know it from looking at their names? Even the people who work in these places often don't know exactly who they're working for – it's not very easy to find out. Why should this be? Who really owns the shops, factories and land where you live?

THE PROPERTY GAME

If you map the buying and selling of property in your local area you can find out quite a bit about what's going on. By looking for FOR SALE signs in the street and advertisements for house sales in estate agents' windows or in the newspapers you can get some idea of the areas where people seem to stay for a short time (frequent sales) and for a long time (few sales).

Which houses change hands most frequently? Are they in a particular area? Do certain types of people live there? What about house prices: are they changing a lot, do they vary according to the different areas or just according to how big the houses are?

Who owns the houses and the land around you? This is often difficult to discover. A lot of property owners don't seem to be very keen on other people knowing who they are. Why? It's surprising how little most people know about this - sometimes it's even difficult to work out who owns the land where your home is located. And what happens if it is up in the air, in a block of flats?

Estate agents, builders, architects, the local housing department, solicitors and several other professions are all involved in the property game, so you might try some of them for information on your local situation.

This could be a start:

QUESTIONS FOR THE ESTATE AGENT

1. Which properties are most frequently up for sale in this area and why?
2. What sort of people buy houses and why?
3. Who are the big landowners in this area and how did they get hold of the land?
4. Why do people want to own houses and land?
5. Why are estate agents necessary?
6. How much money do they charge for their services?

"Look vicar, twenty storeys—you can have the top floor and a penthouse vicarage and we'll make the gravestones into a pop-art mural outside."

A QUESTION OF IDENTITY

The House as a Place
A little
house with
small
windows,

a gentle
fall of the
ground to
a small

stream. The trees

are both close
and green, a tall
sense of enclosure.

There is a sky
of blue
and a faint sun
through clouds.
Robert Creeley

What about your home: is it a house or a flat, do your parents own it or rent it? How long have you been there? How is it different from other people's homes in your street or block? What makes it your place?

At home there is usually family territory. It will be marked by walls and fences, hedges or grass and will be shared by you all. You may also have your own room which you label with posters and other things which identify you with it. From the outside your home may have labels which show that your family lives there.

Things in the garden, a name, a choice of colours which is different from the neighbours, are all your labels. In tower blocks, too, there are ways of showing the difference between flats. Look at the curtain arrangements or the light shining out of the windows at night. Of course, the insides of the flats are very different.

Some sort of local survey will give you a picture of the differences between homes in your area. I've suggested one sort of survey but you could work out other ways of surveying your area, finding out what's there and trying to work out why.

LOCAL HOUSING SURVEY

Choose a number of houses in your area and fill out a sheet for
each. How do they compare?

1. Road/Block....................

2. Number........................

3. Colour of paintwork..........

4. Building materials/walls.....

5. Building materials/roof......

6. Curtain material and
   arrangement..................

7. Garden/Window box............

8. House name...................

9. Front gate...................

10. Wall/Fence/Hedge.............

11. Things in front of house.....

....

....

12. Sketch of house

Rowhedge school
Oaktree Lane
Radley estate
Elmton

This part of the address includes larger places than your desk and the classroom. It fits the school into the town where it is located.

STREET SCALE

Like most buildings, the school is located on a road or pathway of some sort. In this case, Oaktree Lane is one of the roads in Radley Estate which is part of the town of Elmton. This section of the address is almost the postal address for the school – although the Post Office will tell you that something very important is missing. It's something that means a lot to the people who sort letters – ask the postman what it is when you see him next.

Almost without fail, a road will have a label to tell you what it is – the sign with its name on it. There may be other labels as well. Oaktree Lane could have been named after the oaks growing there, and these would be another label, a further piece of information on the place if you couldn't see the sign.

A road is usually owned by the local authority where it is located, but some are private new or unmade roads (sometimes called 'unadopted' roads). In the local council's road you will see lorries and equipment with the council's name and label being used to repair or clean it. The road also has edges which go from the end of the road surface to houses, garden walls or field hedges.

> ### Upgrading
> POOR People's Lane, Mucky Lane, and Backside Lane, all in the parish of Bempton, near Bridlington, Yorkshire, have been renamed. They are now St Michael's Walk, Buckton Gate, and Green Lane.

What do names really tell you about streets?

You have the advantage of seeing the street and the name labels in your home area. But what would you expect the Birmingham streets shown opposite to look like? Do the different kinds of names give you any particular idea about what the area is like or the people who live there? What kind of street name do you associate with what kind of people? Are you right? Get out and find some in your own area.

32

How did these names come about? Some are pretty easy like Barrack Street, a street near an army barracks. Mafeking Road, and Shakespeare Drive will need more than a dictionary, but as a clue, the first was a battle and the second was a person. You could do a history of your local roads – perhaps the first of its kind.

You might also find out how new roads are named. The local council should know.

TOWNPRIDE

If I am in the town where I live and someone asks me where I come from, I tend to give the area or the road – it's likely that local people will know it. But if I'm on holiday somewhere else in the country and someone asks where I come from, the place I usually give is my home town. Towns often mean a great deal to us. Amongst a town's labels it may have a nationally known football team or local hero. When we hear these labels mentioned, we see ourselves as belonging to the same place.

Some towns have rather strange labels. Comedians make jokes about them – Wigan or Scunthorpe, for example.

To get some idea of how your friends see your home town and others, list about ten towns they are likely to know, in alphabetical order, and then ask people to write down what they think of each of them in turn.

The official image of a town. What do these pictures tell you about the way these towns think of themselves? Coats-of-arms and badges, public buildings and other property from the dustcart to the mayor's car, local festivals, fêtes and shows, processions and quaint historical customs – all these go to make up that official image.

You can ask people what they think these towns look like and what sort of feeling they have about them. Compare the results which you and your friends get. Why do people describe places in a certain way? There are no right answers, and no right pictures, but it's interesting to try and work out why towns have the images they do. Often the pictures or images which people have in their heads are very different from the real towns when they see them. What about Oxford, Newcastle, Exeter? They may be even more different from the way the people of a town itself think they should be seen.

It's not really true to say that a town has one owner. Except for a very few places – Bournville, the chocolate town in Birmingham which is owned by the Bournville Village Trust, for example – there are many landowners within a town or city, though not nearly as many as there are people who live there. How would that affect the labels it uses?

When I mentioned hierarchies before, it was mainly in terms of people rather than places. But the same Russian-doll system works when we look at places. The hierarchies by which villages, towns and cities are organized have usually 'happened' rather than been created at one time by someone with a brilliant idea. In your area you may be able to find isolated farms or rural homes which are near a village or small country town. People living in the isolated homes shop in the village and their mail is probably delivered by the village postman. On their address you would probably write 'near' and the name of the village. But the village itself is usually near a bigger settlement which offers more shops or other services. People from the village *and* the isolated homes have to travel to town for banks, government offices, etc. So we have three stages – the isolated home, the village and the town. But then above the town is the city, where things are even more specialized – colleges, medical facilities, important offices – places which the people in the isolated homes visit only occasionally. And among a number of cities in a country there is usually one capital city which is the centre of government and in many cases also the largest and most important city in that country.

WHERE DO YOU FIT IN?

You and other members of your family probably go to certain places for certain things. Draw up a copy of the table below and fill it in. Is there a pattern about these visits?

Reason for visit	Name of the place visited	How far is it from home, in minutes?	How often is the place visited? How many days are there between visits?
A Buy sweets			
B Buy the weekly shopping			
C Visit a large department store			
D			
E			
F			

Think of some more reasons for making useful visits to places and fill in spaces D, E and F.

The place hierarchy seen from the air in the area around Norwich. Can you see the pattern?

Is there a relationship between 'how far you go' and 'how often'? If you live right in the middle of a capital city, you could well 'visit' the city centre just for a packet of sweets, even though it's right at the top of the hierarchy of towns in the country; on the other hand if you live in a small village, you certainly won't be able to visit a large department store there. How can you tell if the places you visit are at the top, middle or bottom of the hierarchy of places? Here's one way: Make a list of the places you visit for A, B and C, and give the places a tick for each of the things you could do there if you wanted. My list would look something like this.

	sweets	weekly shopping	large department store
A Oakwood Road (local shop)	✔		
B Kings Heath (shopping centre)	✔	✔	
C Birmingham City Centre	✔	✔	✔

Places with all three ticked would be high in the hierarchy; those providing only sweets would be low. Try labelling the places you visit 'high', 'medium', or 'low' in a spare column of your table. Why do you think reasons A, B and C were chosen to put in the table?

You can enlarge your list of places and ticks to include your own suggestions for D, E and F. How do these fit into the hierarchy?

Elmton
Essex
England
Great Britain and Northern Ireland

This part of the address goes on to even bigger areas, fitting the imaginary town of Elmton into a county, Essex, and into the larger units of England, and Great Britain and Northern Ireland or the 'United Kingdom'.

COUNTRIES

Most countries, including Britain, have a long history during which they grew from other, smaller areas into large units. As communications developed, so smaller, often self-governing areas joined together or were captured by the people in one strong area.

But for the day-to-day running of a country it is essential to divide the area up again into smaller units which can handle their own affairs through local government, without waiting for everything to be done by a national government. This idea of 'local government' is used throughout the world as a means of organizing people, land and resources especially money from taxes. In England we have a new system of counties and metropolitan counties at the regional level, each including a number of districts at the local level. In the United States there's the same kind of hierarchy, only the names are different.

Similar systems exist all over the world. If you write to the embassy of a country you are interested in, you'll be able to find out how it is divided up, what the areas are called and when they were last altered.

district

Moving up the place hierarchy. Like the distance jumps in the pictures at the beginning of the chapter, each level of organization fits into the next one up the scale.

local area

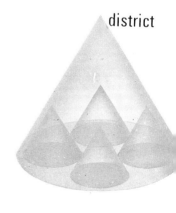

country

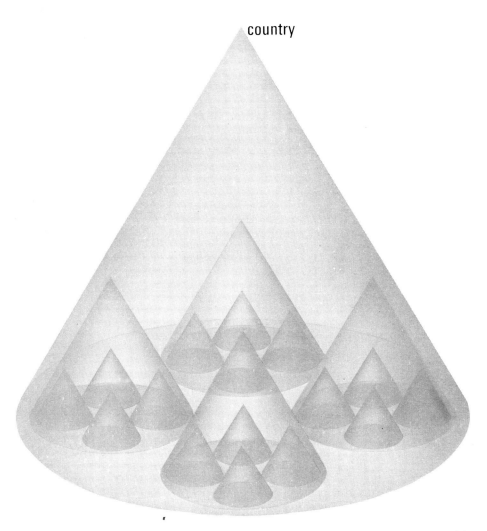

WORLD LABELS

For a long way back into English history, the counties were the main units of local government. At one time they had considerable power. Now, in the twentieth century, the power of the counties has been much reduced by the central government in London, and things associated with counties, like the regiments of the Army, have largely vanished.

Today, the cricket team is perhaps one of the most obvious things attached to the county in Britain. Teams survive even when the counties change – for example there is a Middlesex County Cricket Club, but no county of Middlesex because it was taken into London when our biggest city was reorganized some years ago. After the recent changes in county and local government boundaries (see page 110), no doubt coats-of-arms and other symbols of the old counties will remain too. Do they where you live?

All countries of the world are rich in labels. Because the United Kingdom includes England, Scotland, Wales and Northern Ireland (together with the Isle of Man and the Channel Islands) we have a large number of them.

There is the flag, the Union Jack, for example, which is made up of the flags of England, Ireland and Scotland. There are also many other flags, for counties, cities, army and navy bases and, of course, for the various parts of the United Kingdom. These parts also have national labels or emblems, like the leek and the daffodil in Wales and the thistle in Scotland. There is also the National Anthem, together with a number of other national songs – official and unofficial – that are sung at football games.

Although our labels are fairly old, even the newest countries in the world are quick to collect a set of their own – the flag, the anthem, the national labels and symbols. Like the older countries, they too advertise themselves by exporting well-known products and sending cultural groups abroad. Several African countries, for example, have formed impressive ballet companies which perform all over the world.

Most of us are very curious about other parts of the world. I must be one of the many people who began collections of things which served as labels for other countries:

stamps, coins, flags, foreign newspapers, paper with different languages printed on it, labels from groceries produced abroad, foreign car numbers, pictures of foreign capitals and leaders.

Can you add some more?

You can build up quite a collection by looking through old magazines or finding people who have been abroad and asking them to help you. If you're ever in your capital city, you'll find that most countries have embassies or trade and tourist offices there, where they keep leaflets and other information on their products and activities. You can write to the embassy for details on any particular country.

41

AS OTHERS SEE US

Often the labels which we think are most important in representing our country are not seen as such by people living in countries abroad.

In a survey which I did in Arizona a few years ago, I asked two hundred Americans what they thought of when Britain was mentioned to them; the replies which came out as the Top Ten are all in the picture opposite. Can you work out what they are? Is that really what it's like?

Of course, we could add a lot more things: national air lines such as Britain's British Airways, India's Air India, Israel's El Al, or Australia's Qantas; display teams like the Canadian Mounties, Britain's Highland Regiment bands, or Russia's Red Army Choir.

In the same way as I suggested listing ten British cities earlier on, try this list of countries yourself. Ask other people to tell you the first few things that come into their heads when you mention each country. You could make your own pictures from it.

AS WE SEE OTHERS

	1	2	3	4	5
China					
Mali					
Ireland					
Luxemburg					
France					
Venezuela					
Namibia					
Tibet					
Iran					

Some places are easy. How easy they are depends on how much you know about them, and that often depends on how far away you are. If you live near a place, the chances are that you may know more about it than someone who lives on the other side of the world. So after a while you can begin to guess what people in Britain will say for their easy places – Spain (bull-fighting, sun or wine) or Holland (cheese or windmills). But what about Mali, Indonesia and Venezuela – come to think of it, where are Mali, Indonesia and Venezuela? What sort of labels do we stick on these countries, and how correct do you think they are? And if you lived in Australia, which would be the easy places and which the difficult ones for you?

Europe
The world
The universe

The world map of countries keeps changing as new names appear and others vanish, but the last part of the address in the front of your textbook is becoming increasingly important today. Rapid travel and communication seem to make the world shrink. In Britain you can pick up the phone and dial Italy, Norway or Switzerland. Countries seem to be closer to each other, and although there have always been treaties and agreements to cooperate, we live in an age where world cooperation is of great importance.

LINKS

In the past, Britain was more strongly linked to other parts of the world, which it ruled, than to the rest of Europe, which it didn't. If that address in the textbook had been written by a schoolgirl in Britain in 1930, then she would probably have included 'The British Empire'. Today, areas which Britain once ruled are nearly all independent.

In the same way, there are no longer any French, Dutch or Belgian Empires, but Europe still has very strong relationships with other parts of the world. Some European countries, like Portugal, still exploit territory and people in Africa, while others are still involved with countries they used to dominate.

Britain is part of a Commonwealth, headed by the Queen, and made up of countries such as Canada, Australia, New Zealand, India and Kenya – all once part of the Empire, but now independent. This Commonwealth is a grouping of countries who use English and trade with each other.

GROUPINGS

Now Britain has joined another group, the Common Market – officially called the European Economic Community (EEC). It is a grouping of countries who have banded together in order to help each other. Their governments agree to do some things in a similar way to reduce the barriers between them.

It is difficult to understand what it means to be in the EEC until we are used to it. Eventually it should mean that we can travel between countries more easily and that there will be more French, German, Italian

The British Empire
at its height, 1926.

Britain's changing world
links. How much do you
think these have affected
the way others see us
and we see them?

The British Commonwealth,
1973.

The European Community,
'The Nine', 1973.

and other products sold in Britain, and more of Britain's products sold in other EEC countries. But there will still be many European countries outside the Common Market.

What do you know about the Common Market? What about your parents? Do you think the politicians who have taken Britain into the Common Market should be made to give us all more information on what it means and how it works?

Groupings of countries for economic or defence purposes, like the EEC, exist throughout the world. Most countries have a complicated series of relationships with a number of others. In times of peace they exchange ambassadors, leaders of various countries visit each other and trade is carried on. In times of war the ambassadors come home, the visits stop and trade ceases.

Below: International cooperation between the Chinese and Tanzanian people: together with 35,000 local Africans, as many as 15,000 Chinese workers have been helping in the construction of the 'Uhuru' Railway (the Swahili word for 'freedom'). The line will link Lusaka, the capital of Zambia, with Dar es Salaam, the capital of Tanzania. The Chinese first arrived in 1968 to begin charting the route across the mountains and plains of East Africa. Building began in 1970, and was planned to finish by 1975. But after only three years' labour, the railway has crossed the border into Zambia, and the workers are likely to have finished their task by 1974. Already, as more Africans are trained to do the work, the Chinese are returning home.

BLOCS

Most people see Europe as being divided between two groups of countries, called power blocs, each bloc including a number of independent countries with their own boundaries, labels and government.

Britain is usually seen as part of the 'Western' bloc which consists of 'democratic' countries. Some, like Sweden or the Netherlands (Holland) have kings or queens, and some, like France and Germany, have presidents. Most governments in these countries are elected by a free vote and there are usually a number of political parties.

In 'Eastern' Europe the countries tend to have only one major party, the Communist party. Such countries as Poland, Czechoslovakia and Rumania have a defence and economic relationship with Russia (the USSR), while the 'Western' countries are usually loosely linked with the United States. At one time there was a very strong barrier between Eastern and Western Europe, so strong that Winston Churchill called it the 'Iron Curtain'. In recent years the barrier has been reduced in importance, although the Berlin Wall still separates two halves of one city. You will find Polish and Bulgarian jam and preserved fruits in British shops, and Russian goods can also be bought here.

But Europe is only a small continent when compared with Asia, Africa or Latin America. They also have blocs and other groupings of countries within them.

Overall, it is difficult to understand that there are more than a hundred and twenty countries in the world, each with its own government and ways of doing things. We hear about very few of them and things are constantly changing. But an up-to-date atlas map is an important reminder of the world as it is, rather than as we might think it is.

A WHOLE WORLD?

It is unlikely that there will ever be a single world government, but there are a number of world-wide organizations which help countries to cooperate with each other to reduce the effects of war and disaster, and to spread health and education.

The United Nations Organization (UN) has members from most countries in the world. In its building in New York, some of the problems which develop between member countries are discussed. The UN has no army of its own and can only help to keep the peace when countries ask for it.

Other agencies of the UN are more effective. The World Health Organization (WHO), with headquarters in Geneva, helps to improve world

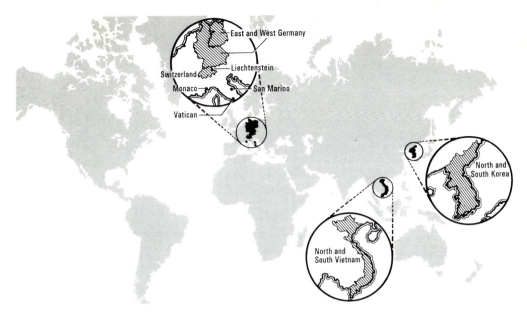

By 1972 all the countries of the world were members of the UN except the ones picked out on this map.

health and living conditions. The United Nations Educational, Scientific and Cultural Organization (UNESCO), with headquarters in Paris, encourages the development of learning, radio and television, and scientific research throughout the world.

Apart from these various organs of the United Nations, there are today[1] some 3000 other listed international organizations, many of which are not fully world-wide, but confined to specific groups of countries having specific common interests . . . they form a very wide variety of working organizations, large and small, covering many aspects of life: politics, trade, travel, trade unions, science, religion, sport, the arts, the professions and hosts of others.

The kinds of planning and organizing that are needed to produce really effective cooperation between nations involve many people. They must travel to conferences, return for consultation[2] with their governments; there must be multilateral[3] consulting; they must gather their facts and seek expert advice. Cooperation is not just a matter of heads of states signing pieces of paper. It involves hundreds of people, separated by hundreds of miles and millions of words.

Colin Cherry, *World Communication: Threat or Promise?*

[1] in 1970   [2] discussion   [3] many-sided

THE UNIVERSE

Twenty years ago, the very last part of that textbook address, 'The Universe', really didn't mean much to most of us. Now it seems to be part of our daily lives. We have seen American or Russian astronauts travelling in space and walking around on the Moon, and we can even accept the idea that men may be on Mars in our lifetimes.

WHAT DOES IT ALL MEAN?

We Earth-men don't seem quick to slice up the Moon or Mars, and claim little patches and put barriers around our plots. True, the first man on the Moon did plant an American flag, but he didn't claim the moon for America as explorers used to do when they 'discovered' parts of the world in the past. The Americans who landed on the Moon saw their job as 'a step forward for mankind'. But what is this 'mankind' of which we are all part?

The trouble with things at this end of the scale – words like 'the universe' which includes everywhere, 'mankind' which includes everyone, and even organizations like the old Empire, the new Commonwealth and the Common Market, is that they are very difficult for most people to understand. Your parents certainly didn't learn about the Common Market in school. But even if you do learn what countries are involved, it's another thing to *feel* that you are part of such an organization. I suppose national politicians and some businessmen who trade around the world do feel that they are in touch with what's going on, but for most of us there is a big space and little else.

We may be aware that these organizations are important, but the spaces and groupings we understand and really feel part of tend to be much smaller, and not usually defined by official boundaries. In fact they are places which only *we* feel that way about and which nobody else sees in exactly the same way. This is what the next chapter is about. It is almost the opposite of the official hierarchy.

3
FEELING SPACE

'So Floppity Bunny ran behind the tree, hopped over the stream and saw the patch of flowers which told him that he was home.'

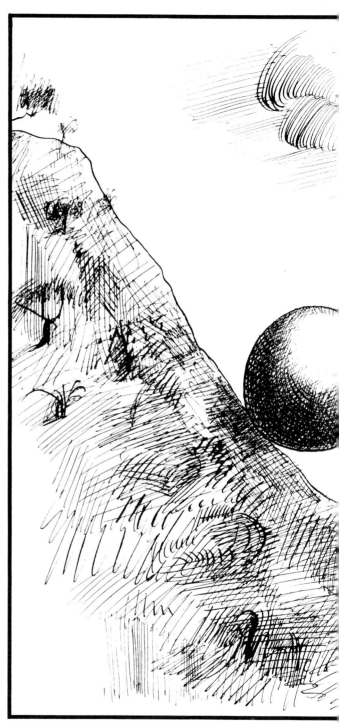

It's a long time since I read anything like that, but now I do remember the way in which animal stories always talked a lot about homes and how safe the area around the home was. They may have been stories, but in fact they were close to the truth. Animals do have areas which they might call 'home' if they could talk. Scientists call these areas *territories.*

Generally, territory bears some sort of relationship to the animal's need for food, or for its bit of space in which to breed and rear its young. In the case of small animals like mice, lizards or inch-long fish, territories need be little larger than about ten square yards. Lions and tigers may need a dozen square miles or more. Generally, the meat eaters have larger territories than the grazers.

Often a territory is shared among several different species. The territory of the swan, for example, is about one-third of a square mile and includes coots, little grebes and gulls, but definitely not other male swans. The squirrel's territory includes hares, woodmice and stags but again definitely not other male squirrels. Similarly the fox tolerates the badger in its neighbourhood but chases away another dog fox. The eagle tolerates small birds, but drives off other eagles.

Some territories are little more sophisticated than a bit of space. Others, as in the case of that of the deer, contain either a wallow hole or a mud bath. Within the deer's territory there will be a fighting ground. There, in the rutting season,[1] generation after generation of rival stags meet. Zebras, too, appreciate the comforts of home. In their case their grooming station is a termite[2] mound.

The peacock has a territory which is as permanent and as elaborate as a medieval castle. Within its territory the peacock has a tree which is used for sleeping, a playground, a sand-bath, a place to eat and a place to rest and, as you might expect, a ground on which it can display its fine feathers. Each of those features is permanent and is used for the same purpose by generation after generation of birds.

How do animals mark out their territory? Dogs aren't very subtle. They simply cock their leg against anything they consider to be their own.

Frank Manolson and Gordon Hard, *Happy Families*

So most animals and birds have these territories. But that word, territory, is still rather hard to understand. Perhaps it is best explained in animal stories?

[1] period before mating   [2] white ant

The mouse child, as he walked backwards, found himself facing the drummer boy. 'Is it really a war?' he asked the little soldier.

'Of course it is,' replied the shrew. 'Our territory's all hunted out, so we'll have to fight the shrews down by the stream for theirs.'

'It's the other way around, the way I heard it,' said the fifer. 'I heard *their* territory's all hunted out, and they invaded ours.'

'What's a territory?' asked the mouse child.

'What do you mean, "what's a territory?"' said the drummer boy. 'A territory's a territory, that's all.'

'Rations don't have territories,' said the fifer.

'Not after we catch them,' said the drummer boy, 'but they do before. *Everybody* does.'

'We didn't,' said the mouse child.

'No wonder you're rations now,' said the little shrew, 'What chance has anybody got without a territory?'

'But what *is* a territory?' asked the mouse child again.

'A territory is your place,' said the drummer boy. 'It's where everything smells right. It's where you know the runways and the hideouts, night or day. It's what you fought for, or what your father fought for, and you feel all safe and strong there. It's the place where, when you fight, you win.'

'That's *your* territory,' said the fifer. 'Somebody else's territory is something else again. That's where you feel all sick and scared and want to run away, and that's where the other side mostly wins.'

Russel Hoban, *The Mouse and His Child*

HOW DOES IT FEEL?

The territory, the home area, what is often called the *neighbourhood* in a city or town, is somewhere that *feels* right. It's all tied up with feeling as though you belong – to the people, to the buildings, to the life there.

Before you read further, make a list or a map of those places where you *feel* right and those places you avoid because you feel wrong. Can you draw a map of the ones in your area?

Marking the feel of a place. Kind ladies love kittens; so a kitten is the sign used by American tramps to point out to other tramps a house in which a kind lady lives. Here are some other signs which these tramps use to chalk on poles, pavements and fences. They make up a whole code for describing the kinds of places they find themselves in. Try inventing some signs of your own.

Kind lady lives here

A gentleman lives here

This community in-different to hobos

Officer of law lives here

No use going this direction

There are thieves about

Keep quiet

Free telephone

Police here frown on hobos

Right: children's territory on the Californian coast.

This feeling of belonging to a place – a territory or neighbourhood – is often very important to people, especially when they settle down or don't have the chance to move about very much.

The Vale of Blackmoor was to her the world, and its inhabitants the races thereof. From the gates and stiles of Marlott she had looked down its length in the wondering days of infancy, and what had been a mystery to her then was not much less than mystery to her now. She had seen daily from her chamber-window towers, villages, faint white mansions; above all the town of Shaston standing majestically on its height: its windows shining like lamps in the evening sun. She had hardly ever visited the place, only a small tract even of the Vale and its environs[1] being known to her by close inspection. Much less had she been far outside the valley. Every contour of the surrounding hills was as personal to her as that of her relatives' faces; but for what lay beyond her judgement was dependent on the teaching of the village school.

Thomas Hardy, *Tess of the D'Urbevilles*

If you think about it, the whole idea of territory was probably much more important to people generally when they couldn't move their homes or even travel into or out of towns and villages so much. People really got to know their home areas and the people around them. They knew a lot about a little, rather than a little about a lot.

[1] surroundings

Battersea

'I never knew an area for being so front-door fixated. People say that there is no place like Battersea for nosey parkers. It was very much the village atmosphere, people growing their tomatoes in the backyards, or keeping their pigeons, to which they were very attached. People respected other people's territory. It had, however, a dingy, a sort of mystical meaning.'

A pub owner

'They used to come here for comfort and companionship. We had a marvellous mix here. I used to say it was where the East End met the West End. You felt that this was where the area sort of came to a head. You knew them, and their sons and fathers, and they all really came together at the annual outing, say, to Hastings or Southend or Brighton. They all mucked in with ten bob to give the older people their day out. It seems daft when you say it now, but everybody knew each other, helped each other out, sort of made it nice. But now? You hear a lot of stories about the new people.'
David Jenkins, *Crack-up of a Community*

The local pub, school or community centre is often like the capital city for a neighbourhood. It can act as a focus for neighbourhood activity and a centre drawing in people from all over the local area for the exchange of information and news.

❝Not everybody would agree with me but I think that the neighbourhood is very important in our lives and will continue to be so.**❞**

61

That's all very well. But what if your area doesn't feel right, isn't a community, or if you just don't like it?

There was no meeting place, no centre, no artery, no organic formation. There it lay, like the new foundations of a red brick confusion rapidly spreading, like a skin-disease.

'But is this place as awful as it looks?' she asked her uncle.

'It is just what it looks,' Uncle Tom replied.

'Why are the men so sad?' she asked.

'I don't think they are that. They just take it for granted . . .'

'Why don't they alter it?' she passionately protested.

'They believe that they must alter themselves to fit the pits and the place, rather than alter the pits and the place to fit themselves, it's easier,' he said.

D. H. Lawrence, *The Rainbow*

Changing it could be one solution. But often, when it comes to altering, planners, architects, politicians – people we tend to see as THEM – are paid to organize things for us, and often they don't seem to know what we really want, which can be just as bad.

It's worth asking some of these people how they decide what's best for you and your family and what information they have to go on.

The estate is a classic example of the pre-war housing development built to cater for overspill population as the initial phases of slum clearance began.

The problems of Wybourn are simple: the area has nothing – few shops, no church, no secondary school, no social centre of any description. True, it has a youth club but this is on the fringe of the estate and many parents will not allow their children to make the hazardous journey to it; within the last month a two-year-old girl was run down and killed virtually on the youth-club doorsteps. Apart from row upon row of terraced housing the only other buildings in the area are three fish-and-chip shops and a large primary school whose amenities (such as they are) are denied the children after four o'clock.

The streets are their only refuge. It is not surprising that petty pilfering is common and the general crime rate extremely high.

The kids' horizons are often restricted within the boundaries of the estate.

Stewart Lowe,
Sheffield Grassroots

What about your area: does it have this kind of problem or does it have places that act as a focus for the neighbourhood where people get together? What kind of places act as centres for you or your parents? Do you feel you belong?

YOU'RE THE EXPERT

Nobody knows <u>your</u> neighbourhood better than you do.
It's something you know more about than any teacher
or any older person. True, there may be the village or
part of town with its history all written up, but that's
not <u>your</u> neighbourhood. True, you may live on a council
estate where you might think the planner who designed
the area knows much more about it than you do. But no,
you are <u>the</u> source of information on <u>your</u> neighbourhood.

   If this is as I believe it is, then let's prove it.
Here is a sketch of <u>my</u> neighbourhood. It's in
Birmingham and I share bits of it with thousands of
people, but the particular area I've drawn here is
unique to me, I'm the only person who sees it exactly
that way.

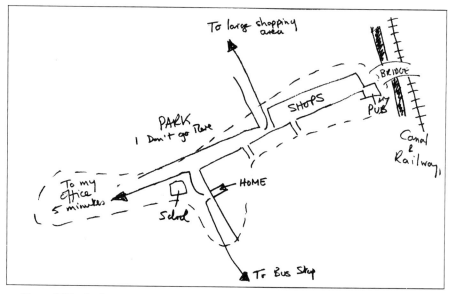

   No official map shows this particular area. It's made
up of bits of several areas marked on the map.

   You can probably draw your own personal
neighbourhood out pretty quickly, but what makes it
interesting is when you compare your map with maps
drawn by friends, family or your classmates. Get them
to put in as much detail as they can, but remember that
the map represents what the person who draws it thinks
and feels about their area. There are no right answers
and nobody has to be an artist to do it. If you compare
a group of these neighbourhood maps with official maps
of your town or village you'll see just how little the
people who draw the official maps seem to know. The
official map world is a different one from ours.

Home territory:
Andrew Storm, aged seven.

67

Feelings about places are built up from our own individual seeing, smelling, feeling and talking. Feelings belong to us alone. But what we tend to do is look for a group of people who feel the same way as we do about an area. Perhaps it's people who have the same interests, go to the same dances or parties, drink at the same pub or play the same sport.

In most countries people play sports based on the neighbourhood. In America the kids play Little League baseball, in France the men go to the park each night to play bowls, and where you live . . . well you know more about that than I do.

Even if you don't actually play any sport, being a supporter of a local team can be just as important in making you feel part of a place. Gangs are often associated with neighbourhoods or local football teams. This is one of the reasons for people belonging to them. Are there other reasons too?

I used to hang around the Collinwood and that with me brother and Pricey and then Ted, and then Bob came 'cause I took 'im from school, ya know like . . . and then a load of different peoples come and go. I mean like if you went round the Collinwood there's all different peoples there . . . went there just to sit around . . . we was only fifteen, we ain't got no pubs or nothing . . . didn't like clubs.

It was a centre weren't it ; it was big flats and all that. I don't know how . . . it just started out of a couple of us going there 'cause some of us lived pretty near there . . . then others started coming over. Only Alan lived on the Collinwood, they all lived around it. Well who goes outside their front door ; if you're going to make trouble ya don't make trouble outside your front door and break your windows and break the people downstairs' to get a complaint about it . . . you'd go over there where there's no one knowing you . . . around the Collinwood there was about twenty on average but with bovver there was something more than that . . . mucking about on the grass and playing football under the light of the pub, about a dozen of us just standing there, just kicking a football all night . . . .

All of the 'ard cases of our time went to the Collinwood about a 'undred of 'em, of which we were the kids, we were the punks, we were the boys . . . we were the boys who thought we were big boys. It was a good place for the summer ; there was a big wall we could sit on and it was near to everybody's 'ouse like, it just caught on. Then it became 'the place', if you wanted to be 'ard then you would go there, everybody knew somebody . . . Skinheads were the big thing.

The Paint House, *Words from an East End Gang*

'PROTECTED' PLACES?

Gangs have a very strong kind of place feeling. They care a lot about 'their' territory and they let everyone know it through their skill with spray cans and by fighting other groups that 'invade' their ground.

You might think that this idea of marking-off a neighbourhood territory is not usually so important to humans as it is to animals. But really it is, and it's not just gangs of young people who go in for it.

It is difficult to believe, but in 1932 the people who lived in a private estate in Oxford built a high wall with spikes on top to keep out the people who lived in a council estate next door. The people in the private estate wanted to keep people in the two different types of housing, the two neighbourhoods, apart. That wall, called the Cutteslowe Wall, was only pulled down in 1959.

If you live in a smart housing area, then your territory may have all been marked out for you already and you could even hire private security men to protect your home ground. If you put up a guarded gate on the edge of your estate and have the money to do it properly, it's not thought to be wrong. But if you do it with a spray can, you'll probably get described by local papers and by magistrates as 'anti-social'.

Keston Park Estate

We have a few estate rules – close-boarded fencing is not allowed, we don't permit trees to be cut or lopped and residents are expected to keep their washing out of sight. Wireless aerials are banned too – but we don't bother about that so much now. There are people who still want to live in nice surroundings . . . the only way to maintain quiet is to be tough with the people who try to nip through.

Sunday Times Magazine

Different kinds of marked-off territory. But how different are they and why are they marked off?
Far left above: gang space, Birmingham
Top centre: doorkeeper, Albert Hall Mansions, London
Above: Keston Park Estate, Locksbottom, Kent
Middle centre: the Bishops Avenue, London
Left: the Cutteslow Wall, Oxford

Rich and poor, private estate and council estate, seem to share the desire to keep the neighbourhood as it is, to preserve those surroundings in which they feel good. Most people are like the squirrel or the fox. They don't mind other people using the neighbourhood so long as they don't cause trouble. But some people, from the red-faced country landowner to the football gang, want their areas all to themselves. Why? Well, it could be because they are afraid others will take it away from them; what do you think?

On the upper West Side, the rental agent of Park West Village 'Your Own World in the Heart of New York', on whom I have foisted myself as a prospective tenant, tells me reassuringly 'Madam, as soon as the shopping centre is complete, the entire grounds will be fenced in.'

'Cyclone fences?'

'That is correct, madam. And eventually' – waving his hand at the city surrounding his domain – 'all that will go. Those people will go. We are the pioneers here.'

But . . . people seem to get used very quickly to living in a Turf[1] with either a figurative or a literal fence, and to wonder they got on without it formerly. This phenomenon was described, before the Turf fences came into the city, by the *New Yorker,*[2] with reference not to a fenced city but to a fenced town. It seems that when Oak Ridge, Tennessee, was demilitarized[3] after the war, the prospect of losing the fence that went with the militarization drew frightened and impassioned protests from many residents and occasioned town meetings of high excitement. Everyone in Oak Ridge had come, not many years before, from unfenced towns or cities, yet stockade life had become normal and they feared for their safety without the fence.

Just so, my ten-year-old nephew David, born and brought up in Stuyvesant Town, 'A City Within a City', comments in wonder that anyone at all can walk on the street outside our door. 'Doesn't anybody keep track whether they pay rent on this street?' he asks. 'Who puts them out if they don't belong here?'

Jane Jacobs, *Death and Life of Great American Cities*

---

[1] territory [2] an American magazine [3] the army base was moved

CHOOSING YOUR FRIENDS

First impressions can be very misleading. How much does your first sight of a person really tell you about them? How much depends on *what* you look at first? Cover up the opposite page and look at the details below. What do you think the owners of these bits are like? Now look at the pictures on the other page. Are they as you thought?

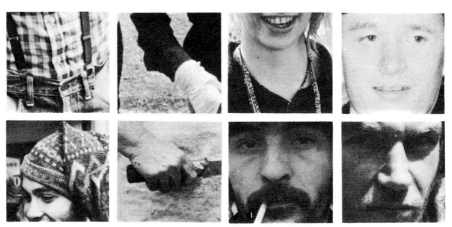

It comes back to the way we choose to be with people who feel the same way as we do, who share the same neighbourhood. This choosing of people goes on all the time in our lives and not just in our local area, either. We all tend to classify each other in order to make describing people easier. Even without talking to someone we pass in the street, we collect quite a lot of information about them. It's not something we usually give a second thought to. It all happens so fast.

Try an experiment and see if you can pin down what goes on. Try to work out exactly what *you* do when you pass or meet a stranger for the first time. What do you feel about them? Do you think they're the kind of person you like? Do you want to know more about them or do you just want to get away as fast as you can? What are the things about them that make you feel this way?

The next few pages are about some of the guidelines that I use. How do they compare with your findings? What order of importance would you arrange them in and is there anything I've missed out?

Sex

Was that a man or a woman, a girl or a boy? I check the face, the shape and the clothes. Once I have decided, I may already feel I know quite a bit about the person because I assume that they share certain

74

things and activities with other men and women. Of course, there are a lot of changes taking place and women are doing more of the things that only men used to be able to do. There are women prime ministers and women jockeys, for example; so I may get it quite wrong.

Age

Another thing we tend to look for in people we pass or meet is their age. We don't usually ask them, we just guess, and the way we guess depends on how old we are ourselves. In Britain people tend to live a long time so a man may not think he is 'old' until he is seventy, but in a country like Indonesia where people do not live so long, a man of fifty may be described as 'old'. If somebody is about your age, then are you more interested in them than if they are much older or much younger?

Appearance

Does the person 'look' like you or does he or she 'look' different? We rely a great deal on what are called 'appearances' – clothes, the way a person walks, the way they decorate themselves or their clothes, what they are carrying and – of course – the colour of their skin and the type of face and hair they have.

Unfortunately, we tend to get confused by two different types of 'appearance' – the things people can change and the things they can't. Unless there is something medically wrong with it, you are unlikely to change the shape of your nose. It is something that you are born with, like the colour of your skin. These things we can't change and probably shouldn't want to anyway.

What we do change is the way we decorate our bodies – with clothes, make-up and jewellery. We use these things to make us different from other people . . . or perhaps to show that we belong to a group of people who share similar ideas to ours. There are thousands of 'uniforms' in the world. Some of them are official ones and some are uniforms which people wear because they want to. As you pass men and women in the street, you learn a lot from the clothes they have chosen to wear. You learn about their sex, their age, and perhaps about the organizations they belong to.

In most countries the appearance of a person also tends to tell us something about their wealth and their job. Appearances can be very deceptive, but if you see a man in a bowler hat, a dark suit and carrying an umbrella, you may think he is 'posh', has a lot of money and an important office job. This could be true, but on the other hand he may have spent all his money on this 'uniform' and his children could be underfed as a

National costumes are a special sort of uniform, but how often and where do you see people dressed in them? Is there an international costume?

result. The point is that we tend to describe people by their clothes and go no further. We might learn a lot more if we asked them about themselves.

Language

If you ask someone what he does and where he comes from and he just stands and stares at you or says something that you don't understand, it's likely that he's speaking another language. If you can find out what that language is, you may know where he was educated. This is really all you will find out, because languages do not tell you where a person was born or where he lives.

If this man replied to you in French, you might think that he came from France. But he could be from Canada or from many countries in Africa. If a girl spoke to you in Spanish, she could be from Spain or from Peru, Argentina, Arizona in the United States, the Philippine Islands or many other places. Most of the world's major languages are spoken in several countries, and to confuse things further, some countries have several languages.

The language, or languages, a person speaks will have a considerable effect on what he learns and how he learns it. One of many reasons why we seem to know so much about America but so little about China is that we share a language with America, but few of us can understand Chinese.

la Suisse French
die Schweiz German
Svizra Romance
Svizzera Italian

The different language areas of Switzerland.

Religion

Religion, too, can play a very important part in the lives of people, and can affect their daily lives. If you look around you, the number of churches in your area or town should give you some idea of how important religion was in the lives of people there when the churches were built. Do you think it is still as important today? Why do the shops close on Sundays? Why do the Jewish ones close on Saturdays? In other parts of the world religion has much more effect on daily life than it does in Britain. It can affect the clothes you wear, the days you work, the shape of towns, how people entertain themselves and what they learn.

You don't need to look further than Northern Ireland to see that religion can also be used as a way of dividing people who live in a country. Some countries, like Pakistan and Israel, were created so that people who shared a common religion could try to prevent disagreement and conflict with others by having a separate country of their own.

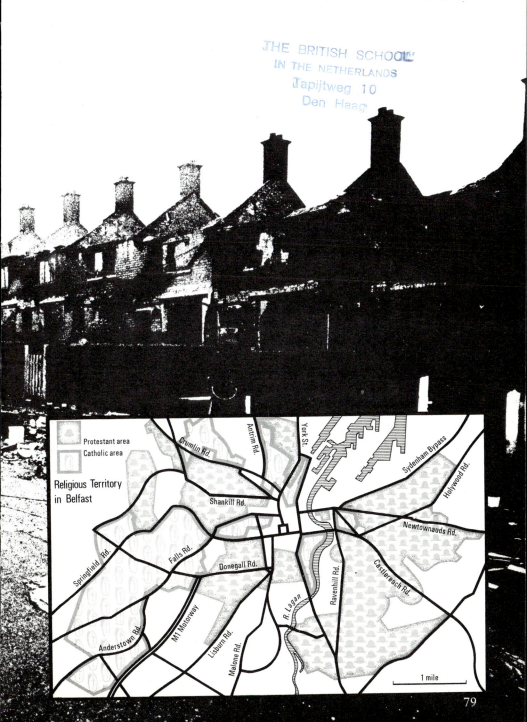

Politics

There's one more feature of the way people are grouped and the way we sum them up that we should look at here – one thing that you can't tell from looking at a person.

If you look at a map of the world, it is not so much that the people over the world are different, but rather that the difference is in the governments which they decide to have to run their countries. Chapter 2 should give you a start, but you'll have to do quite a bit more chasing in reference books to find out what each of the governments does.

One thing I think you will find soon after you start looking is that those governments seem to be very proud of their countries. They act rather like you or I and seldom admit that they are wrong. They always seem to see only the best side of themselves and reject people outside their group. It's a bit like local-gang-feeling about people and territory, only on a much larger scale.

Different blocs, but the same feeling?
Above: display at Pyongyang's stadium, North Korea. It reads 'Long live the people of Unified Korea'.
Top right: Independence Day Celebrations – a gigantic American flag made in Manchester, New Hampshire, USA in 1914.
Right: General Bokassa, President of the Central African Republic, visiting General Amin of Uganda.

This national pride is probably a useful thing when it allows people
to feel that they belong to a larger group – that they have fellows who
think and behave as they do. But it is a dangerous thing as well, leading
to wars which people who are not involved can often see little reason
for.

81

A CHANGING WORLD

In the twentieth century, we have seen some very great changes in the world map because of wars, when one country wants more land or wants to control the people of another. This happened in the two World Wars of 1914–18 and 1939–45, and still happens today. You probably know of wars which are happening as you read this. How much are they to do with national pride?

1947 U.N. RECOMMENDATION

Damascus
Mediterranean Sea
SYRIA
ISRAEL
Tel Aviv • Jerusalem
Suez Canal
JORDAN
Cairo •
EGYPT
SAUDI ARABIA
Red Sea

1949 ARMISTICE LINES

Damascus
Mediterranean Sea
SYRIA
ISRAEL
Tel Aviv • Jerusalem
Suez Canal
Cairo
JORDAN
EGYPT
SAUDI ARABIA
Red Sea

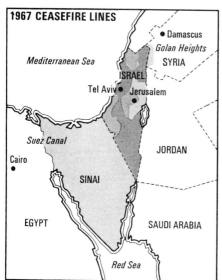

1967 CEASEFIRE LINES

Damascus
Golan Heights
Mediterranean Sea
SYRIA
ISRAEL
Tel Aviv • Jerusalem
Suez Canal
Cairo •
JORDAN
SINAI
EGYPT
SAUDI ARABIA
Red Sea

1973 CEASEFIRE LINES

Damascus
Golan Heights
Mediterranean Sea
SYRIA
ISRAEL
Tel Aviv • Jerusalem
Suez Canal
Cairo •
JORDAN
SINAI
EGYPT
SAUDI ARABIA
Red Sea

There's another kind of change that has affected the map of the world in the twentieth century. But it's not something you can easily see on the maps. It's more to do with how the way we feel about places is affected by time and distance.

Paris is 1100 kilometres from Rome. That's a long way if you have to walk, go by car or even by train, but if you can get there in an hour by plane, is it really so far away? Or if you can telephone your friends there as easily as your friends on the other side of your home town, are they really so far away? Really, the distance between places may not matter too much, it's the time and money it takes to get there that is most important.

What about your world? Try drawing a map of your area in terms of time and distance. Work out how long it takes you to get from one place to another. Draw a map of these places using a scale of five minutes (instead of so many metres or kilometres) to ten millimetres.

Knocking holes in the map: an advertiser's view of the way fast train services change the 'real' distance between one place and another.

Over the world as a whole, air travel has made the passage of many things much quicker than before. Ideas – in the heads of men and women – can pass rapidly over continents, but so can disease. A plane only has to take on infected food or water somewhere and a disease can spread across the world in hours rather than the weeks or months of a few years ago.

In Britain our own lives are increasingly tied to the lives of people in other parts of the world. We receive information about them in the papers and on TV and radio, and we travel much more.

This is only part of the story, though. There may have been great advances in communications, but this doesn't mean that we get to hear about everything that goes on in the world.

You may remember that when I talked about the Common Market in Europe I said that our government seems to tell us very little about what is going on. If we don't get told much about our own country, you can bet we hear even less about other countries. This is especially true of those in Africa and Asia: when did you last hear about Gabon, Cambodia, Costa Rica? How many countries of the world do you really know anything about?

Below: what do you get to know? The BBC brings the world's news to people in Britain, but in 1973 it had news correspondents only in these places. Does this affect the kind of world news we get?

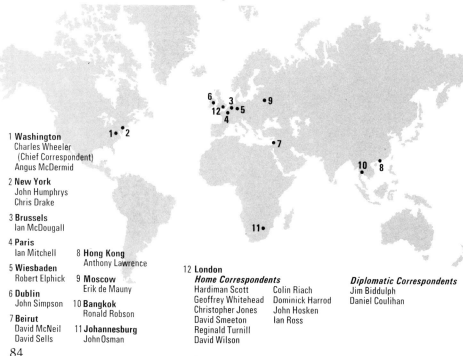

1 **Washington**
Charles Wheeler
(Chief Correspondent)
Angus McDermid

2 **New York**
John Humphrys
Chris Drake

3 **Brussels**
Ian McDougall

4 **Paris**
Ian Mitchell

5 **Wiesbaden**
Robert Elphick

6 **Dublin**
John Simpson

7 **Beirut**
David McNeil
David Sells

8 **Hong Kong**
Anthony Lawrence

9 **Moscow**
Erik de Mauny

10 **Bangkok**
Ronald Robson

11 **Johannesburg**
John Osman

12 **London**
Home Correspondents

Hardiman Scott	Colin Riach
Geoffrey Whitehead	Dominick Harrod
Christopher Jones	John Hosken
David Smeeton	Ian Ross
Reginald Turnill	
David Wilson	

Diplomatic Correspondents
Jim Biddulph
Daniel Coulihan

84

WHAT DO YOU KNOW?

You can get some idea of how this affects what we know and think of other countries by watching the news on TV or listening to the radio news for a week. Each time another country is mentioned, write it down. If, for example, France is mentioned six times in one news broadcast, it would score six for that day. If you add the scores for each country at the end of the week, you will get some idea of the way in which TV and radio provide us with information about the world.

You will probably find that some parts of the world, like Africa, Asia and South America, tend to score rather low. Why is this? Is it because nothing happens there? Is it because Britain is not interested in these areas? Or is it because the people who prepare news broadcasts don't think we want to know what happens there?

MENTIONS ON LONDON TV NEWS FOR ONE WEEK

AREA OF WORLD	MON	TUE	WED	THUR	FRI	SAT	SUN	TOTALS FOR WEEK
England	20	15	14	23	12	17	8	109
Ireland	7	8	—	3	5	—	6	29
Scotland	2	3	—	—	1	2	3	11
Wales	—	1	—	—	1	1	—	3
Europe								
France	3	—	—	2	1	—	—	6
Germany	4	2	2	—	—	—	—	8
Spain	—	1	—	—	—	—	—	1
etc.								
United States	4	6	7	3	—	—	2	22
Canada	1	—	—	—	1	—	1	3
Brazil	—	—	1	—	—	—	—	1
Russia	4	2	2	1	3	2	1	15
India	—	1	1	—	—	—	—	2
China	2	1	1	—	2	—	—	6
Israel	—	—	1	2	—	—	—	3
South Africa	—	1	—	—	—	1	—	2
etc.								
MENTIONS TOTALS FOR EACH DAY	47	41	29	34	26	23	21	

You could do the same kind of experiment to find out what <u>kinds</u> of news we get to hear about and what kinds we don't.

All these things affect our opinions and how we feel about places and people we don't know. Our feelings about our neighbourhood territory are formed by our experience there, but what about our feelings and attitudes towards the rest of the world? A lot depends on the experience we get through the television and the newspapers. Travel costs money and so it is only usually the people with money who manage to travel freely and find things out at first hand. Or people with employers who will pay for them to travel.

But there is another, slower kind of movement of people around the world, which is also very important. It is like a continuous exchange of people from country to country, though not always an equal exchange.

This process has gone on for many years. In the nineteenth century shiploads of British people went to live in America and Australia, and many people still go to these and other countries every year. Now too, scientists, teachers and businessmen go from Britain to countries that need them or will pay them well to come, while people from other countries come here to work, often on our transport system and in our hospitals. In Europe there are Yugoslavs working in Germany, Spaniards in Switzerland and Algerians in France. The Chinese run shops in Singapore, and Asians have been the shopkeepers and businessmen in many African countries.

CHANGING PLACES

One in every ten workers from North Africa, Turkey, Yugoslavia, Spain and Greece earns his or her living in the richer countries of Europe. In 1973 the United Nations estimated that there were eight million migrant workers in Europe. These pictures show people from Spain and Algeria moving north to France and Switzerland in search of work, and passing through immigration control for admission to their 'new' countries. Many of them have had to leave their families behind in order to come and find jobs.

Gen Amin gives more than 8,000 British Asians two days to leave Uganda

Above and right: Far from home. Temporary accommodation in the new country while proper homes are found: Asian families try to settle in Stradishall Camp, Suffolk.
Below right: a family in their new home.

Not all such movements are made because the people concerned want to. Some governments force certain groups of people to leave their country and others will not allow all people to come in. In 1972 Asians were forced to leave Uganda and many came to Britain. Few of them wanted to leave Uganda, where they were born and had good jobs, but the government there forced them out. Wars also have the effect of forcing people to leave their homes, which may be destroyed or be ruled by a new government. The word *refugee* makes me think of hungry people without homes, people who have had no say in where they are to go.

The result of movements over the years has been that people from one country can usually be found in another. They may keep the passport of their old country, and as long as they do, they probably feel that they really belong to their old country. They will pay taxes in their new country, but probably will not vote. On the other hand, they may become citizens of their new country, learn the language, exchange their passport and gradually adjust to life there: making friends, marrying and eventually feeling totally a part of their new home.

This change of countries is a slow process, but it does happen to many people. It may have happened to you, to some people you know or who live in your local area. How does it feel? Find out where other people have come from, and why; what they do here, whether they are happy and how difficult they have found it to adjust. They can tell you a lot more about what it's like in the places they have come from than television or your geography books will. They may also give you a new view of your own place and life.

As people move about the world and settle in different countries, so other things tend to go with them. Look around you. We have a number of such things in Britain – Chinese, Indian, Italian and American restaurants and take-away foods, Sikh temples, West Indian music, and words from many languages.

Words in our language reflect this. American words are especially common. Why do you think this is? 'Disc-jockey' (DJ), 'teenager', 'baby-sitter', 'commuter', are all from the United States and you can probably think of many more. 'Bungalow', the word for a one-storey house, came from India in the last century. 'Trek', a slow difficult journey, comes from South Africa. The 'anorak' jacket is an Eskimo word which came to us from Denmark. What about 'au pair girl' and 'discotheque', 'scampi' and 'robot'? Where did they come from?

The same thing happens all over Europe, with English words in French and Russian, for example. The effect is to reduce differences between countries and peoples. Although we may feel that we want to identify clearly with a place or a specific group, this does not mean that we should not share the words and ideas from other countries.

Any one place is a mixture of people and things from lots of other places. But often we don't realize the opportunities offered on our own doorstep. You may not be able to afford to take a jet trip round the world, but if you look around, you may find that the world has come to you.

How much is one country really one country? As people come and go they leave their imprint on their surroundings. How many different communities can you see here? . . . and around you?

4

MANAGING SPACE

What happens when you go to another country?
As Britain is an island, you can't just drive up
to the border as most people do in Europe. You
have to go by sea or air.

At the port or airport in Britain, a passport
with your name on it is shown to an official and,
in a way, he lets you out of the country. Actually
he is checking to make sure that you'll be able
to get in again. When you reach the country you
are going to, you'll have to show your passport
to somebody who is at your 'port of entry'. If this
is a seaport, like Le Havre in France or Esbjerg
in Denmark, then it will really be on the 'edge'
of the country, on the boundary. But if you travel
by air, you will only show your passport when
you land. The airport may be in the middle of
the country and you will have crossed over the
'edge' sometime before. Because of the
development of rapid sea and air transport,
boundaries at the 'edge' of countries are less
important today than they were in the last
century, or even when your parents were born.

Going through border control at Marseilles, France.

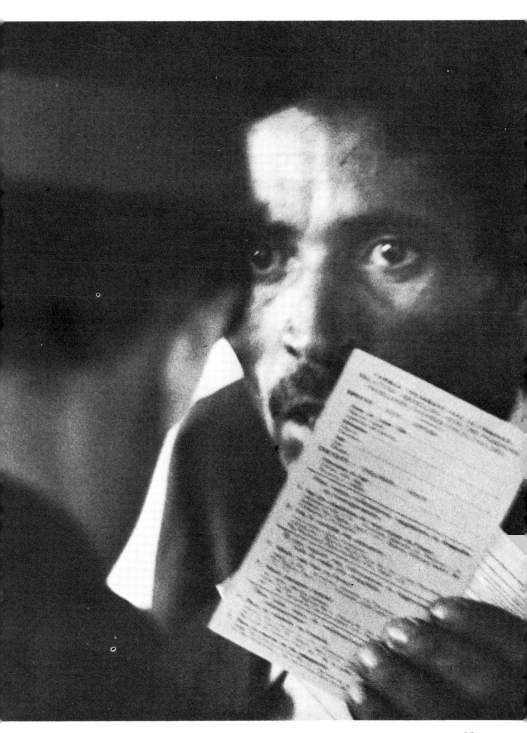

This is a very long way from the original territories which our ancestors held, where the boundaries were known but were not marked. The Bushmen of South West Africa probably show us how we once functioned:

Although Bushmen are a roaming people and therefore seem to be homeless and vague about their country, each group of them has a very specific territory which that group alone may use, and they respect their boundaries rigidly. Each group also knows its own territory well; although it may be several hundred square miles in area, the people who live there know every bush and stone.

Thomas Marshall, *The Homeless People*

Very few parts of the world operate like this today. Though we still have very strong feelings about our personal and neighbourhood territory, the formal organization of space, involving boundaries and governments, doesn't take much notice of those feelings at all. 'Civilization' has brought with it rigid boundary lines and special groups of people who manage space on behalf of the rest of us.

BOUNDARIES BETWEEN COUNTRIES

Take national boundaries: originally most boundaries between countries were zones or frontiers. They were strips of land, often quite wide, where two countries met. In some remote parts of Africa or Latin America there are no real boundaries today, and you would have to look at your map to see if you had passed from one country to another.

What originally made countries mark boundaries, and often put up some sort of barrier, was the threat of invasion. Some of these barriers are very old – like the Great Wall of China, or the Roman Wall in northern England.

The Roman wall is an impressive frontier defence in northern England, near the Scottish border. It was constructed after the Ninth Roman Legion had been defeated in battle by people from south-west Scotland. The massive wall was backed to the south by an occupied zone from which the natives were excluded.

Frontiers are usually in lonely areas and the soldier's life is dull . . . except when the attack comes. Perhaps this is how the Roman soldier might have felt as he looked north from the wall:

The Great Wall of China. This huge wall runs
nearly a tenth of the way round the earth.

Roman Wall Blues

Over the heather the wet wind blows,
  I've lice in my tunic and a cold in my nose

The rain comes pattering out of the sky
  I'm a Wall soldier, I don't know why.

The mist creeps over the hard grey stone,
  My girl's in Tungria; I sleep alone

Aulus goes hanging around her place
  I don't like his manners, I don't like his face.

Piso's a Christian, he worships fish;
  There'd be no kissing if he had his wish.

She gave me a ring but I diced it away;
  I want my girl and I want my pay.

When I'm a veteran with only one eye
  I shall do nothing but look at the sky.
W. H. Auden

Because boundaries were established for defence, rivers and mountain ranges were often chosen. The trouble is that it is difficult to actually mark a boundary in a river and rather difficult to string one out along the tops of mountains. Often people just had a rough idea of where the boundary was, and so long as there was no trouble between neighbouring areas, it was not marked or clearly drawn on a map.

In 1965 Indiana and Kentucky, two neighbouring states in the United States, tried to decide where the boundary was between them. The line was somewhere in the Ohio River and after a great deal of thought,

The committee has unanimously agreed that, after extensive research, there is no physical basis for determining the boundary, no definite points of reference ever having been established.

Louisville Courier-Journal

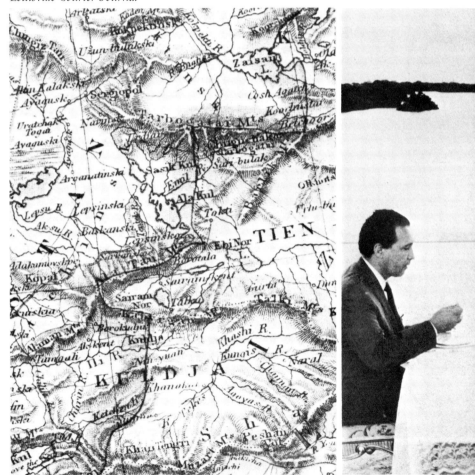

Where a river does form a boundary between countries, the best idea is usually to agree that the boundary should run down the middle of the river. As rivers flood and dry up, it is often difficult to decide where the middle is, but if two countries decide on where they think it is, then they can mark the boundary on bridges.

Below left: mountain boundary between Russia and China as shown in an atlas of 1883. But what would it be like on the ground?

Below: 1967, President Carlos Lleras Restrepo of Colombia and President Raul Lenoni of Venezuela have a discussion over lunch without either of them leaving their own country. The boundary runs across the bridge, over the table, and down the centre of the river separating their two countries.

WHAT KIND OF BOUNDARY?

Boundaries come in all shapes and sizes. Some are very well defended while others are easy to cross. This rather depends on the countries involved. If you look at the map, you will see that the United States has two very long boundaries, one in the north with Canada, and one in the south with Mexico.

The northern boundary runs through farming and wooded areas in the main and, although there are customs posts on the roads which cross it, there is no fence; not much more than a ditch in most places. It would seem that there's no great problem about the movement of people between the United States and Canada.

But on the southern boundary which the United States shares with Mexico, things are very different.

Right: the great lengths the US authorities are prepared to go to in order to stop people crossing the Mexico-US border illegally.

Below: the US-Canada border. In places it is even more open than this.

THE United States-Mexic border begins in the qui surf of a beach seven mil west of San Ysidro. Fro there, where Mexicans an Americans alike enjoy uni hibited Sunday walks, th border climbs, dips and rur eastward — 1,945 mile through mountains, desert canyons and rich agricultur lands to the Gulf of Mexico.

It is, whether marked b the brown curl of the R Grande or by occasion scatterings of chain lin fence, a border, not a barrie in the physical sense. Alon the greater portion of i route, there is no sign of th boundary at all, just periodic stone monumer erected between the two cou tries by some forgotten su veyor. There are some chec points or ports of entry which all legal entries mae by car or on foot must, b law, take place. But they ar mere dots on the large expanse of territory " shared by the two countries.

The rest of the border i for all practical purpose wide open. There are tw main traffic funnels—bot legal and illegal—from the in terior of Mexico into th United States : through E Paso for Mexicans bound fo Denver and points east, an through San Ysidro for th majority of those bound fo California.

It is the urban and there fore more anonymous spraw of the San Diego—and, ulti mately, Los Angeles—are which attracts most aliens Once across the border, th illegal alien has stretching be fore him Interstate Highway and US Highway 395—twi paths to the heart of what h sees as a motherland o American jobs. And once in land, he has a good chance o losing himself in the imper sonal throb of Mexican-Ameri can city life or the quieter but safer rôle of the field hand.

Making it safely to the California interior provides other safeguards against de portation. If successful in ob taining a job—and forged documents that usually satisf

Robert Kistler on another American 'war'

Artful dodgers

Cut wires on the Mexican border

an employer are available on both sides of the border—the illegal alien has a reasonably good chance of going about his new life without detection.

He also quickly acquires " human equities," or life ties, which may make deportation unlikely. With life comes love, marriage, perhaps children, a boss who might step forward to plead his case, even a creditor or two who may ask the Immigration and Naturalisation Service to forego deportation—at least until the new television set is paid for.

For all these reasons, the border patrol makes its most determined stab at curbing the flow of illegal aliens at the border itself. The Chula Vista sector headquarters of the border patrol is a few miles north of the San Ysidro port of entry. The sector, one of 22 such jurisdictional areas in the United States, is responsible for 70 miles of border watch, from the ocean east to the Imperial County line.

Chula Vista sector officers caught, and returned to Mexico, 73,115 illegal aliens in the year—a staggering statistic given the unique combination of rugged terrain and numerous urban hiding places in the San Ysidro area.

And what about those who got away ? How many thousands did they total ? According to Richard Batchelor, Deputy Chief Patrol Agent for the sector since 1961 and a border patrolman for 31 years : " No one really knows. We by no means get them all, because about 2,000 wets (wetbacks) who say they came across in our sector are caught each month by various immigration investigators throughout the country.

" If I had the responsibility of mounting an old-fashioned sweep of the Los Angeles area for aliens tomorrow the only thing that would limit the number of illegals I could catch—for a few days, anyway—would be the amount of rolling stock I could get my hands on to cart them away."

INS estimates of the number of illegal aliens in the Los Angeles area vary, but most officials say publicly their number probably exceeds a quarter of a million. But for Batchelor and his men. those aliens are someone else's problem. At Chula Vista sector headquarters, the Los Angeles illegal immigrants are past history—those who made it through one of the most sophisticated human and electronic " catch " systems ever devised.

The border patrol is understandably reluctant to discuss its surveillance system in detail. Where the sensors are and how specifically they work is closely guarded. There are several types of the devices : those which detect the passage of a human body by its heat ; those which react to the presence of metal and those which magnify sound to the extent that a well-trained operator can hear footsteps (and guess the numbers of persons involved) miles away.

Of course, the entire border is not plugged into the surveillance network. That, according to Batchelor, would be impractical if not unworkable. There are just too many aliens going across the international line at too many places for any number of border patrolmen to keep up with.

The modern border patrolman is also helped by sophisticated devices like night field glasses. He has the use of helicopters and fixed wing aircraft piloted by highly specialised officers. Yet, with all of the sophistication, the battle often comes down to a footrace.

Carl Fisher, a border patrolman for seven years, has a zeal for his job that cannot be faked, but also a basic, underlying empathy for the aspirations of the men he is chasing. " You can't get down on the average wetback," he says. " He's just a poor guy trying to do his best with his life. Most likely, he's an honest man who probably works harder for his bread than most Americans. Like as not, he probably sold everything he owned or borrowed from every relative he had to get his chance to be smuggled across.... " — Los Angeles Times.

PLANE WRECK AT LOS GATOS

The crops are all in and the peaches are rott'ning,
The oranges piled in their creosote dumps;
You're flying 'em back to the Mexican border,
To pay all their money to wade back again.

Chorus *Goodbye to my Juan, goodbye, Rosalita,*
Adios misamigos, Jesus y Maria;
You won't have your names when you ride the big airplane,
All they will call you will be deportees.

My Father's own Father, he waded that river,
They took all the money he made in his life;
My brothers and sisters come working the fruit trees,
And they rode the truck till they took down and died.

Some of us are illegal, and some are not wanted,
Our work contract's out and we have to move on;
Six hundred miles to that Mexican border
They chase us like outlaws, like rustlers, like thieves.

We died in your hills, we died in your deserts,
We died in your valleys and died on your plains,
We died 'neath your trees and we died in your bushes,
Both sides of the river, we died just the same.

The sky plane caught fire over Los Gatos canyon,
A fireball of lightning, and shook all our hills,
Who are all these friends, all scattered like dry leaves?
The radio says they are just deportees.

Is this the best way we can grow our big orchards?
Is this the best way we can grow our good fruit?
To fall like dry leaves to rot on my topsoil
And be called by no name except deportees?

Woody Guthrie

Right: 1970. The plight of the migrant
farmworker hasn't changed much since
the song above was written in 1948.

There are some boundaries that are almost impossible to cross unless you have a very good reason to go to the next country, but most are fairly easy if you are not smuggling something in with you.

While they can be rather frightening if they have armed guards on them, in other cases they can be places where people meet with welcome signs and tourist shops at the border, the national flag, and their first sight of signs written in a foreign language.

How much do borders tell you about the relations between the countries on either side of them?
Right: Germany (Berlin) East and West, 1964.
Below: France and Belgium, 1969.

WHO OWNS THE SEA?

These days when we use the sea and the air as well as the land, there are other national boundaries, apart from the land borders, which a country has to control. This doesn't mean that it stops people crossing them, but rather that it puts certain limits on the way they do so.

It was originally to catch smugglers that most countries with sea coasts extended their boundaries into the sea – usually five kilometres from the shore. There was obviously no line in the water, but there were maps, and within this limit coastguards and customs men could search boats and ships suspected of carrying out illegal activities. Most of the sea is still not 'owned' by anybody, but fish is becoming an increasingly important and valuable world food, and as supplies have become scarce in some places there have been battles about which countries' boats can fish where, and the five-kilometre limits have been extended by many countries.

There are other reasons too. Below the sea which surrounds Britain there is a ledge of seabed called the continental shelf. For a long time no one took much notice of it, but when oil and gas were found in the North Sea, Britain, Norway and other countries who had bits of coast bordering on the North Sea, divided up this continental shelf so that they could explore it. They also made a lot of money by selling the prospecting rights to oil companies. Like all such agreements between countries, the line was carefully mapped to avoid disputes.

Channel boundary line snags

By Roger Vielvoye

Attempts by Britain and France to fix a boundary line dividing their offshore territories in the English Channel and Western Approaches have run into difficulties.

There has been a broad measure of agreement over the line down the centre of the English Channel, but problems have arisen over the position of the Channel Islands.

Because of the inability of the two countries to fix a median line in this area it has not been possible to decide on the boundary line in the Western Approaches.

While there are a number of interesting exploration prospects in the eastern end of the English Channel, the density of shipping in these waters would make offshore drilling a hazardous business.

Rig operators have pointed out that some ships have found it difficult to avoid running into well marked and established hazards in this area, and there is considerable doubts about their ability to spot and avoid drilling rigs, which move to new locations every few months.

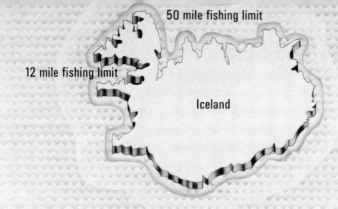

50 mile fishing limit

12 mile fishing limit

Iceland

WHAT'S THE LIMIT?

1. There's money in the sea. Fishing is Iceland's main industry, and fish and fish products make up 80 per cent of its exports. When catches are poor its whole economy suffers. In 1970 there was a crisis of this kind. For years modern, efficient trawlers from Iceland, Norway, West Germany, Russia and Britain had been fishing at such a rate that the herring couldn't breed fast enough to replace their numbers. The cod, too, were in danger, and the catches poor. In 1972 Iceland extended her territorial waters from 19 kilometres to 80 kilometres off her coast (from the 'twelve-mile' to the 'fifty-mile' limit) to try to protect the fish breeding grounds and limit the catches by only allowing Icelanders to fish there. The fishing fleets of other countries strongly opposed this, particularly the British Trawler Owners Federation, as Iceland is one of their nearest and richest hunting grounds. They would rather let the future take care of itself than sacrifice their livelihoods to Iceland now. How should the sea be divided up?

2. There is money under the sea too, but there are no limits to the ownership of the seabed when it comes to oil. The United Nations 'Convention of the Continental Shelf, 1958', divided the seabed among the countries bordering it by drawing an imaginary line *halfway* between their coast lines, and giving them the right to do as they liked with their side. Some of the European countries concerned immediately started selling 'licences' to companies for the exploration of the seabed. In 1965 the first off-shore gas field was found and in 1967 the first oil field.

As more discoveries were made, and it became clear that there *was* oil, a great rush began. The British Government was criticized by some people for charging too little for their licences – £45 per square kilometre of the sea bed and then £50 a year plus $12\frac{1}{2}$ per cent duty on each barrel of oil landed. So they *auctioned* the next set of licences and Shell Esso paid £21 million for one site alone.

But unlike the fish, which could replace their numbers if enough of them were left to breed, the oil is non-renewable and will eventually run out. A large well will produce oil for an average of ten to fifteen years. North Sea supplies may only last for twenty-five years, and in thirty to forty years at the most the whole industry will have packed up and left.

How then should the sea be divided?

Undersea Oil Boundary

Norwegian Area

Denmark

Danish Area

12 Mile
Fishing Limit

German Area

Dutch Area

Netherlands

British Isles

Belgian
Area

Belgium

France   105

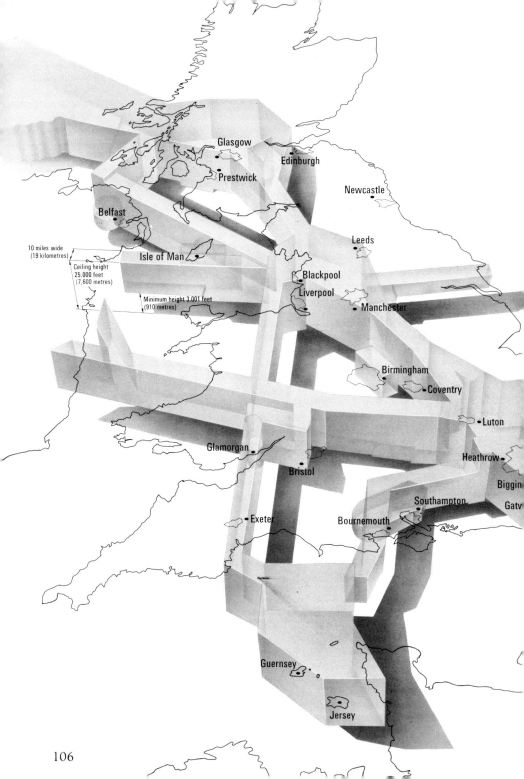

Glasgow

Edinburgh

Prestwick

Newcastle

Belfast

Leeds

10 miles wide
(19 kilometres)

Isle of Man

Ceiling height
25,000 feet
(7,600 metres)

Blackpool

Liverpool

Minimum height 3,001 feet
(910 metres)

Manchester

Birmingham

Coventry

Luton

Glamorgan

Heathrow

Bristol

Biggin

Southampton

Gatv

Exeter

Bournemouth

Guernsey

Jersey

DIVIDING THE SKY

There are boundaries in the air too. Countries started making rules about this a long time ago when there were balloons rather than aeroplanes:

In 1785 an American, John Jeffries, and a Frenchman, François Blanchard, crossed from Dover to Calais by balloon. Naturally it was not long before aviation began to be exploited for military purposes. In the French Revolutionary Wars captive balloons were used for artillery spotting, being employed even as far afield as Egypt. The Austrians tried bomb-laden balloons at the siege of Venice in 1849, but most of these were carried away from the target. Some even drifted back and exploded over the Austrian lines. Balloons were also used at Solferino in 1859, and again in the American Civil War [1861–5]; but not to much effect. sensation was caused when Gambetta and over a hundred and fifty persons escaped from Paris in balloons during the Franco-Prussian War [1870–71].

D. H. N. Johnson, *Rights in Air Space*

Well, this was in the days when balloons just floated, not like modern aircraft which can be controlled very carefully to avoid accidents. Nobody can paint lines on the clouds, but because of the very large number of aircraft using the air above countries like Britain, there have to be rules and regulations about where they fly.

Britain's airways.

At a big international airport like London's Heathrow there are almost 500 planes taking off every day and as many landing. To make sure that the aircraft are safely separated and not delayed there are Air Traffic Controllers who channel them along the 'corridors' known as airways, which are shown here. The pilots navigate along these routes with the help of radio beacons and directions from the controllers on the ground, who track their flight with special equipment. The controllers make sure that the planes are not less than five miles away from each other in distance and a thousand feet in height, and stop them straying from the airways. But the areas between the corridors are also important, being used by the military for experimental, testing and training flights, and civil aircraft are not allowed to fly in them without permission, just as the military aircraft are not allowed to use the corridors for their experiments. No doubt they have their own maps dividing up the sky.

BOUNDARIES INSIDE COUNTRIES

Boundaries *inside* countries serve a slightly different purpose from the ones which separate countries, but everybody seems to use them.

Looking back into history, when cities were much more powerful than they are today, you find that many cities had edges to keep their population and animals safe from people outside. In history there have been many occasions when cities have been attacked, often by people from other cities. Walls and castles remind us of this today. Many of Britain's old towns – York, Totnes and Londonderry, for example – have the remains of city walls or gates which were built to protect them. Each city was virtually a separate country, and these barriers worked in the same way as boundaries between countries.

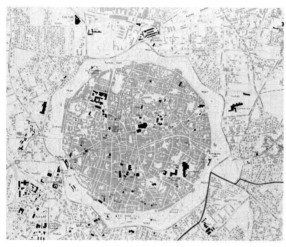

The eastern part of Nicosia, capital of Cyprus. Though the city has outgrown the old boundary walls, they still show very clearly on the map.

Today cities and towns do not need to protect themselves in this way and have usually expanded far beyond the old walls. The boundaries inside countries that matter now are the lines established by national governments in order to make their job of governing easier – the local government boundaries.

These are less well marked than the boundaries that mark the edge of the country. You don't need a passport to cross them, in fact in Britain the chances are that you won't even notice you have crossed one. Their main function is not to control the movement of people, but to make management of space inside the country easier. In order to govern efficiently, a government must be able to collect rates and taxes, and provide services like education, sewers, water and a thousand other things. And when there are so many people, it helps to divide them up into groups according to where they live, to make these jobs easier. I talked about this earlier, in Chapter 2, and about the hierarchy of divisions within any country (see page 38). Laws can be very different on either side of this kind of boundary in some countries. For example, if you travel across the Washington–Oregon state boundary in the United States, the driver announces, 'smoking is not permitted on board this bus in Oregon.'

But because the boundaries are often poorly marked, people sometimes build houses on them and problems can result, as this letter to the governor of an American state suggests:

Dear Governor,

I have a question which I wish you would answer for me. My house is located near a point where three county lines meet. My dining room, where I eat, is located in Nicholas County. My bedroom, where I sleep, is located in Fleming County. My mailbox is located in Robertson County.

I have lived in this same house for twenty years and have always voted in Robertson County. They have taken my name off the list of registered voters claiming that I do not reside in Robertson County.

Please tell me where I am entitled to vote, if you can.

Louisville Courier-Journal

Don't think that this can't happen in other countries too. Until recently there was a lady in England who lived on the boundary between the counties of East and West Suffolk. She paid taxes for her kitchen, dining room and scullery, three bedrooms and bathroom to one office, and taxes on her drawing room, study and four other bedrooms to another office.

"Art thou trying to start another War of t'bloody Roses, Mr. Walker? Your new Yorkshire-Lancashire boundary goes right through my parlour."

One of the reasons for this kind of confusion is that the boundaries are often very old and many changes have taken place since they were marked. People often forget why the boundary was put there, and believe that it should last forever. As patterns of where people live, how they move about and their ways of doing things change, so boundaries inside countries may have to change in order to work properly.

In 1973, the local government structure of England began to alter. Some of the old county names went and many other counties changed their size and shape. When the reorganization is complete, the total number of local authorities will be reduced from 1243 to less than a third of that number. The same thing has happened in other countries, like Sweden and France. But to understand what happened in England you will need to compare the old with the new maps.

Britain before and after the local government reorganization.

1 Northumberland
2 Cumberland *
3 Westmorland *
4 *Cumbria*
5 Durham
6 *Tyne & Wear*
7 Yorkshire *
8 *Cleveland*
9 *North Yorkshire*
10 *West Yorkshire*
11 *Humberside*
12 *South Yorkshire*
13 Lancashire
14 *Merseyside*
15 *Greater Manchester*
16 Cheshire
17 Derbyshire
18 Nottinghamshire
19 Lincolnshire
20 Shropshire
21 *Salop*

22 Staffordshire
23 Leicestershire
24 Rutland *
25 Herefordshire *
26 Worcestershire *
27 *Hereford & Worcester*
28 Warwickshire
29 *West Midlands*
30 Northamptonshire
31 Huntingdon
   & Peterborough *
32 Cambridgeshire
   & Isle of Ely *
33 *Cambridgeshire*
34 Norfolk
35 Suffolk
36 Gloucestershire
37 Oxfordshire
38 Buckinghamshire

39 Bedfordshire
40 Hertfordshire
41 Essex
42 *Avon*
43 Wiltshire
44 Berkshire
45 Greater London
46 Surrey
47 Kent
48 Cornwall
49 Devon
50 Somerset
51 Dorset
52 Hampshire
53 Sussex *
54 *West Sussex*
55 *East Sussex*
56 *Isle of Wight*

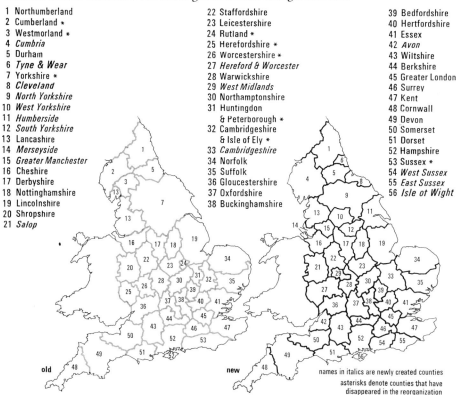

old   new   names in italics are newly created counties
asterisks denote counties that have disappeared in the reorganization

In England, the central government believes that the new pattern of local government will allow for the better organization of public services. Because there will be fewer local government districts with more people in each, they will have more money from rates and taxes to provide services. After a period of confusion, while people try to work out what their new address is and to whom they write letters to complain about services like education, planning and health, the government hopes that the new units will permit the more effective use of public time and money.

UNWANTED BOUNDARIES

Boundaries which are built to separate people who may not want to be separated are annoying, and are not usually the best solution to a problem. The strange thing is that as we are learning that they are not very useful things – except for managing space – new walls and barriers are being built. Have you tried to cross a motorway except by a bridge? You'd probably be run over before crossing one lane.

Motorways can be new barriers to our movement. They're supposed to speed journeys up and break down the barrier of distance, for people who have cars anyway. But in the process they can also cut through the city and countryside and divide people who used to meet together. Often they break up neighbourhoods and limit movement. How would you deal with this problem? Are there other new barriers too?

Bristol's 'Berlin Wall'

The carriageways will be laid down within 50 ft of the walls of modern tower blocks of flats.

The flats, built in 1968 in full knowledge that the road was coming in 1972, will suffer high noise levels and all the blight a multi-lane highway brings with it.

The corporation planning depart-ment is trying to reduce the road's impact. A 10 ft high solid barrier will be built along each side, pedestrians wil be funnelled under subways, and there is great play with shrubs such as cotoneaster and climbers such as Virginia creeper.

On the ground-floor flats in adjoining blocks like Vinings

Walk, tenants are undecided whether the 10 ft barrier will be better or worse than the noise it is designed to reduce. 'It'll be Bristol's own Berlin Wall,' said Mrs V. R. Davis, aged 68. 'My husband has lost a leg, he can't get about. He spends all day look-ing out of the window. This baffle will cut him off from the world.'

INVISIBLE BOUNDARIES

Managing space would be a relatively simple thing if it were only a matter of national boundaries and local government areas. Most people at least know that these things exist. But there are other boundaries – lots of different ones, possibly more than ever before – that organize our lives and manage the space around us, and because they're usually invisible most people don't even know they're there.

In fact a lot of people have their own set of boundaries within which they work. Your school probably has what is called a *catchment area,* the area where children in the school come from. If there isn't a map already, the easiest way to find it out is to get all the students in the school to mark where they live on a map of the area and then to draw a line round the edge that includes everyone. The area inside that boundary is your school catchment area, though you'll probably find that there are a few people who have some special reason for being at your school, who upset the neatness of the pattern. Your local education authority or the schools themselves can probably give you an idea of how other schools in the area fit into the picture.

As with all the other 'invisible' boundaries, it's always worth asking who decided on that particular area and why. You may have a better idea.

There are lots and lots of these boundaries and areas. The milkman has a 'round' which can be mapped and which includes those streets which he serves. The postman is the same, and the code numbers which we are supposed to put on letters are the numbers for each area. There are the public services: the gas board, electricity board, fire brigade (if there's a fire at your school, which fire station will the fire engines come from? And at your home?) hospitals (if you're knocked down in the street or taken ill in one place, which hospital will the ambulance take you to?) and every kind of private business too.

How do these boundaries work? Take the postman, for example. He can only visit a certain number of houses a day, so his boundaries include the right number of houses. The same is true of the milkman, paper boy, gasman and everybody else who serves your home.

One of the London Electricity Board's invisible boundaries appearing thanks to a strike. In the power-workers strike of 1970 electricity supplies became so short that they had to be rationed. Here some areas have had their power cut off while others blaze with light.

The size of the territory will depend on how many places the person has to call at, how, and how fast they can get round. For the postman on foot it is small, while a man delivering soft drinks from a van might have a very large territory. He can move fast and may not have many stops. The main thing to remember is that each person's boundaries are different, and they are kept in their heads or marked on maps rather than on the ground.

Postmen collect their letters from a post office, milkmen load up at a dairy, paperboys collect papers at a newsagent. Each post office, dairy and newsagent has a number of people carrying goods out to the surrounding areas. If all the areas served by each person are added together, a much bigger area will be covered on the map.

It's the hierarchy system again, and it is the way most organizations manage space. Looked at from the top end, they probably have a head office and then a number of smaller offices, each with its own territory.

Imagine a company producing clothes, with its main office in London. It will probably have a number of salesmen driving around trying to convince shopkeepers that they ought to stock these clothes. Each salesman will have an area of the country to work in and he may have other men working for him with even smaller territories on which to concentrate. The boundaries of these areas may be marked on maps rather than on the ground. They are also likely to change if the company wants to sell more clothes or starts producing something else.

Most of these 'invisible' boundaries are marked on maps belonging to the particular company concerned, and exist to help them divide up space so they can get their business carried out as efficiently as possible. Although it's a neat system of dividing up space for the people who do the dividing up, it's not always so helpful for those on the receiving end.

Take the hierarchies in the way goods are sold. Someone in your house buys a transistor radio and it stops working three months later. They take it back to the shop and the shop says that it must go to the factory. The shop sends it, but the factory doesn't mend it, sends it back and it fails again.

It is often difficult to find out who to complain to. The person who buys the radio feels lost and powerless. There are now laws to help this person – the consumer – to act. One way is to write to the owner of the company that produced the radio. A better way is to go to the local citizen's advice bureau.

Then there's politics. Your family is represented somewhere on your local council by someone, even if nobody in your house voted at the last local election. This person has a territory which is full of people he or she represents or serves. Have you seen your local councillor lately? Do you know who he or she is?

The country is also divided up so that people can elect Members of Parliament (MPs), one for each area. Your family has an MP who should sit in Parliament in London and pass on your ideas to the other MPs. Do you know who that person is? Do you know if they do their job properly?

One trouble is that too many people give up too easily. If something happens to disturb them – trees are cut down in the local park, cars are dumped on their street or the police pick on a noisy gang of kids who are not really breaking the law – people just moan and don't (or don't know how to) do anything about it.

Do we have the power to change these things? Do you think people like you, your parents and friends, use what power they have enough? Are you going to help change things?

114

WHICH SIDE HAS POWER?

5

OVER TO YOU

A lot of this book has told you what I think about things and my way of ending is to hand over to you. This is probably not very fair, but I'm doing it because there just are no final answers when you look at things like place, boundaries, countries and the other ideas that have appeared in this book.

All I've tried to do below is to suggest one or two subjects which you might consider and do something about.

1

The first thing is to think about the many needs which we have as human beings. Earlier on I wrote about our need for the friendship and closeness of other people like ourselves – this idea of feeling right with people in a place. But we also know that there are times when we want to be alone. So ideally we need a place where we can both meet people and be alone if need be.

This is a matter of *balance*, of weighing one thing against another. Take the point about territory. We all probably like to have a patch of land or a space somewhere that we can call our own. But we also like to visit other places. If everybody put up massive barriers around their territories, there would be nowhere for us to visit. So again the issue is balance ... keeping the boundary big enough so that we can feel safe, but keeping it small enough so that most people can get in to see us.

2

The second thing which I think is worth thinking about is knowing places.

Nothing beats going to see places. If you really want to use this book then you have to go off in search of some of the things that I mention and you'll certainly discover much more than I know about.

We all have very small ideas about the world around us. You may think that because I've written a book about places, I know a great deal. But there is a way of proving that that's not true.

Maps like this one show the *bias* which a writer has with regard to the world, the way he sees it without perhaps realizing that he doesn't see it as it is in the atlas.

The map of the text of the book. With the help of the picture list on page 125 try doing your own map of the pictures of this book. How does it compare with the map of the words?

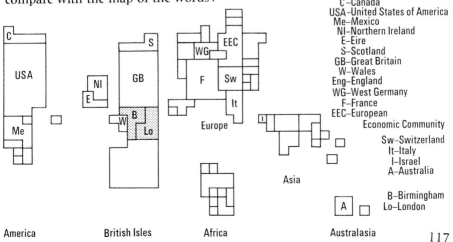

C – Canada
USA – United States of America
Me – Mexico
NI – Northern Ireland
E – Eire
S – Scotland
GB – Great Britain
W – Wales
Eng – England
WG – West Germany
F – France
EEC – European Economic Community
Sw – Switzerland
It – Italy
I – Israel
A – Australia
B – Birmingham
Lo – London

America   British Isles   Africa   Australasia   117

YOU CAN PRODUCE A MAP LIKE THIS

All you need is the newspaper or book you're checking, a large piece of graph paper with small squares, a pencil and quite a bit of time.

If you take a newspaper, read through the whole thing - every page and every line - and make a mark on a piece of paper each time a country or a place in a country are mentioned. The following paragraph on the 1972 Olympic boxing would score:

Britain-1; Hungary-1; Kenya-1; Mexico-1.

Britain's other quarter-final contestant, Maurice Hope, the welter-weight was outmanouevred by Kajdi, the Hungarian. Kajdi meets in the semi-finals Dick 'Tiger' Murunga, the Kenyan, who knocked out his Mexican opponent in the first round.

When you've gone through a whole paper you will have a very large number of references. Probably Britain will be up in the hundreds.

The best way to carry on is to look at each country in the atlas and then to cut out of the graph paper the right number of squares - one for each mention - in roughly the right shape.

It takes a while to get the shapes looking something like the countries but if you have them cut out, you can shift them around on a board or table until they begin to look right. When they look OK, stick them down and write the names on some or all of the blocks of squares.

You can do the same thing with a local paper and see how much bias there is towards certain towns in your home area.

You can also do it with papers from different cities in England.

The maps opposite show what happens when you do this sort of mapping exercise for two newspapers published in different cities on the same day. The things that had happened in the world over the past twenty-four hours had provided the news for each of the papers, but their coverage is very different.

The Times in London mentions more places more times and covers more countries in Asia and more counties in England (I've included counties and some cities on these maps).

The *Birmingham Post* has less coverage throughout the world, the blocks for most countries are smaller than for *The Times*. The fact that the *Birmingham Post* is a thinner paper is partly the reason, but the *Post* really is more a local paper.

Look at the number of mentions for Birmingham (B) in the *Post* and the number of mentions for Birmingham in *The Times*. Now look at London – the positions are reversed.

Map of *The Times*
Monday 29 June 1970.

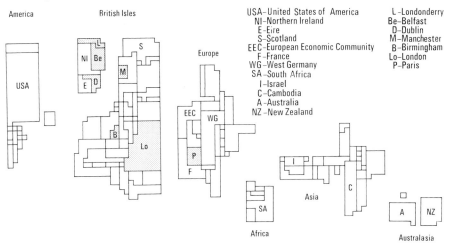

Map of the *Birmingham Post*
Monday 29 June 1970.

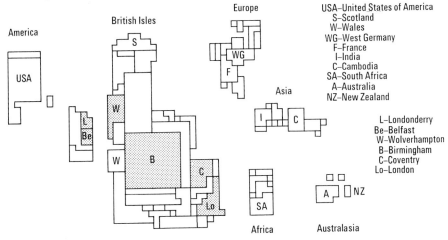

One major thing which we can learn from these maps, and from the map which I have drawn of this book, is that in Britain we hear far too little about other parts of the world.

This is really a circular process which is very difficult to break.
We hear little about most foreign countries
And so
We have little information to keep us interested in them
And so
Newspapers don't include so much information on foreign countries as they don't think we are interested
And so
We hear even less about most foreign countries
and so it goes on, unless we choose to do something about it.

3

The third thing that comes up from this book concerns war and conflict. Perhaps it is because there are always wars going on around us, but I haven't mentioned them that much in the chapters above.

We always tend to blame wars – even little ones in the family – on somebody else. When it comes to the big international wars, then we usually sit back, watch people get killed on television, and blame 'Them' for starting the trouble.

Unfortunately we are all 'Them'. When I wrote about boundaries, barriers and territories, I suggested that we all had them. Like animals, we all defend them too. This can easily lead to conflict, but at the local, neighbourhood level people don't often get hurt. Conflicts over territory can even seem funny.

But wars are not funny when they lead to the deaths of hundreds or thousands of people, people who are very much like you and I.

An awful lot of television seems to be concerned with violence and force, with wars and experience of wars. Like me, you probably get sucked in and enjoy a good Western, or a serial based on the Second World War. But remember . . . war can be injurious to *your* health.

A True Story
Postmaster Bradbury of Leeds had just finished smoothing the cement of his forecourt when Chip, a local dog, trotted across it.

Mr Bradbury warned Chip off, re-smoothed his cement, and was easing his back when Chip did it again.

Mr Bradbury hurled his shovel at Chip, following it up with a kick. The kick landed on Mrs Rowley, Chip's owner.

Mrs Bradbury, who had observed the incident, decided to call the police. A similar decision was taken by Mrs Rowley.

Mrs Bradbury reached the telephone first. She dialled the first three nines when Mrs Rowley pulled her out of the box by the hair.

While settling their differences both ladies fell into the cement.

It was at this point that Mr Bradbury's mother-in-law, Mrs Stevens, decided to intervene. Both she and Mr Bradbury were pulled into the cement by the infuriated wives.

Mrs Stevens is in her late eighties.

Outraged at the behaviour of his neighbours towards his wife, Mr Rowley charged across the road and carried Mr Bradbury and himself back into the cement.

All five voters then waded into the cement and each other.

The Magistrate, Mr Walter Smart said:

'You'd better forget the whole thing.'

Christopher Logue, *Private Eye*

4

The fourth thing which I have mentioned in this book concerns something which I think you can do something about. Remember I talked about our need for places that we know well and *feel* good in?

Well, looking around you, it must be pretty obvious that many people's places are vanishing. It may have happened to you or your family.

When a house or a neighbourhood is threatened with demolition, it's not just buildings that are going, but people's territories as well.

You can act to save such places. The main thing is to find out what is happening in your local area. Read the papers and notice boards. Try and get the facts from teachers, friends and others who may know. Go and ask the people who are planning to destroy or change an area what they are doing and why they are doing it. They may try and turn you away, but you do have rights.

Often people are successful in saving what they value – it can be done if you work with your neighbours and don't give in to 'Them'.

They Are Tracking Down Everything Picturesque

gentlemen came with portfolios[1] and measuring rods
they measured the ground spread out their papers
workers shooed away the pigeons
ripped up the fence tore down the house
mixed lime in the garden
brought cement raised scaffolding
they are going to build an enormous apartment house

they are wrecking the beautiful houses one by one
the houses which nourished us since we were small
with their wide windows their wooden stairs
with their high ceilings laps on the walls
trophies of folk architecture

they are tracking down everything picturesque
chasing it away persistently to the upper part of the town
it expires like a revolution betrayed
in a little while it will not even exist in postcards
nor in the memory or souls of our children.

Dinos Christianópoulos

[1] briefcases

122

5

The last thing I want to say is the 'where do we all go next' type. It's all very well for people like me to write books and suggest that you do things to change the world around you, but it's much more difficult for you to actually make the changes.

This book has really been about *place* and that's the thing I want to end on. You have to work out in your mind – perhaps not yet, but sometime – whether you believe and feel that places are important. Many people would say that with our modern way of life, places don't really matter. I don't agree with this, but I've included a poem which explains why some people have given up believing in *place*.

I still think that you and I need pieces of this earth where we feel good, pieces of earth which we feel we belong to and can have a say in changing. If nobody cared about place or places, then buildings could be knocked down in all directions, roads could cover every field and nobody would care enough to do anything about it.

I don't want to live in that sort of world.

'It Must All Be Done Over . . .'

Wherever I look the houses are coming down,
the yards are deserted,
people have taken to tents and caravans,
like restless cattle breaking stride,
going off with their wagons
under a rumbling cloud.

I have begun to believe those rumours
of the world's wheat being eaten
by metallic grasshoppers,
 and columns of brutal strangers
advancing on the soul of Asia.

I hope I shall be able to leave
without too much baggage
or bitterness. I must make my life
into an endless camp,
learn to build with air, water and smoke.

John Haines

INDEX OF THEMES

While reading this book you may find that there are certain ideas or themes in it that you want to explore further or base a project on. Many of them appear again in the other books in the *Human Space* series. This index is to make it easier to follow up ideas *across* the series in this way. It doesn't attempt to be a comprehensive guide to everything that appears in the books, or every aspect of the themes listed. Instead it offers some pointers and some possible lines to work along.

You will find the same themes listed at the end of the other books in the series – UTOPIA, SURVIVAL, EXPLORATION and MAPS – giving the relevant pages to follow up in each. This should make it possible to pursue any of these themes across all five books and to use each book in a number of different ways. There is other follow-up material, ideas, book references and information in the *Human Space* handbook and the Games and Simulations book.

LIST OF ILLUSTRATIONS

ACKNOWLEDGEMENTS

14   *Account of the History, Manners and Customs of the Indian Nations* by
        John Heckwelder, American Philosophical Society 1819
30   'The House as a Place' by Robert Creeley from *Words: Poems by Robert
        Creeley*, Charles Scribner's Sons, N.Y. 1967
36–7   'Where do you fit in?' Material contributed by Roger Robinson,
        Birmingham College of Education
49   *World Communication: Threat or Promise?* by Colin Cherry, Wiley –
        Interscience 1971
54   'Happy Families' by Frank Manolson and Gordon Hard, the *Observer
        Magazine* 17 January 1971
55   *The Mouse and His Child* by Russell Hoban, Faber & Faber 1969
59   *Tess of the d'Urbervilles* by Thomas Hardy from *Existence, Space and
        Architecture*, Studio Vista 1971
61   'Crack-up of a Community' by David Jenkins, *The Times* 6 July 1970
62   *The Rainbow* by D. H. Lawrence, Estate of D. H. Lawrence and
        Laurence Pollinger Ltd
64   'Wybourn' from *Sheffield Grassroots* by Stewart Lowe, G. Green
69   *The Paint House* by P. McGuire, Penguin Education 1972
71   'Keston Park Estate' *Sunday Times Magazine*
72   *Death and Life of Great American Cities* by Jane Jacobs, Random House
        1961
94   *The Homeless People* by Thomas Marshall, Knopf 1959
95   'Roman Wall Blues' by W. H. Auden from *Shorter Collected Poems
        1927–1957* Faber and Faber, Random House Inc
96   'Kentucky-Indiana Row: Physical Basis Lacking for Boundary
        Decision' *Louisville Courier-Journal* 19 April 1966
99   'Artful Dodgers' by Robert Kistler, Los Angeles Times/Washington Post
        News Service
100   'Plane Wreck at Los Gatos' by Woody Guthrie, music written by
        Martin Hoffman, Tro-Essex Music
107   *Rights in Air Space* by D. H. N. Johnson, Manchester University Press
        1965
109   'Dear Governor' a letter from an article by Ray Coons from *Louisville
        Courier-Journal*
121   'True Stories' by Christopher Logue, *Private Eye*, 12 September 1971
122   'They are Tracking Down Everything Picturesque' by Dinos
        Christianopoulos in *Modern European Poetry* by Willis Barnstone
        et al., Bantam Books 1970
124   'It Must all be Done Over' from *Stone Harp* by John Haines, Rapp and
        Whiting